WRITING
RESEARCH
PAPERS

A Guide
to the Process

WRITING RESEARCH PAPERS

A Guide to the Process

STEPHEN WEIDENBORNER

DOMENICK CARUSO

St. Martin's Press   New York

cover photo: Matthew Klein
cover design: Melissa Tardiff
typography: James Wall

cloth ISBN: 0–312–89499–6
paper ISBN: 0–312–89500–3

Acknowledgments

"Davis, Jefferson" reprinted with permission of the *Encyclopedia Americana*, Copyright 1980 by The Americana Corporation.

"Jones, Mary Harris" reprinted by permission of the publishers from *Notable American Women, 1607– 1950*, edited by Edward T. and Janet W. James, Cambridge, Mass.: The Belknap Press of Harvard University Press, Copyright © 1971 by Radcliffe College.

Excerpts from *The Readers' Guide to Periodical Literature*, Copyright © 1977, 1978 by the H. W. Wilson Company. Material reproduced by permission of the publisher.

Excerpt from *The New York Times Index* for 1977 © 1977 by The New York Times Company. Reprinted by permission.

Helmut A. Abt, paragraph from "The Companions of Sunlike Stars." Reprinted with permission from *Scientific American*, April 1977.

Malcom W. Browne, "Arguing the Existence of ESP." © 1980 by The New York Times Company. Reprinted by permission.

Lawrence K. Altman, "Senility Is Not Always What It Seems to Be." © 1977 by The New York Times Company. Reprinted by permission.

Walter Sullivan, "New Clues to Animals of the Ice Age." © 1978 by The New York Times Company. Reprinted by permission.

"Cassatt, Mary" reprinted with permission from *The New Columbia Encyclopedia*. Copyright © 1975 by The Columbia University Press.

Emily Dickinson, "Poem 1475," reprinted by permission of the publishers and the Trustees of Amherst College from *The Poems of Emily Dickinson*, edited by Thomas H. Johnson, Cambridge, Mass.: The Belknap Press of Harvard University Press, Copyright © 1951, 1955 by the President and Fellows of Harvard College.

Emily Dickinson, "Poem 406." Copyright 1929 by Martha Dickinson Bianchi. Copyright © 1957 by Mary L. Hampson.

Contents

Preface   ix

1 AN INTRODUCTION TO THE PROCESS   1

Some Essential Definitions   **2**
An Outline of the Research Process   **3**

2 DEFINING YOUR OBJECTIVE   5

Choosing a Subject   **5**
Choosing a Topic   **6**
Forming a Hypothesis   **18**
Some General Reference Sources   **21**
Review Questions   **25**
Exercises   **26**

3 USING THE LIBRARY   31

Working with Librarians   **31**
Kinds of Sources   **32**
The Library Card Catalog   **33**
Locating Books   **36**
Periodical Indexes   **38**
Types of Periodicals   **39**
Indexes to Popular Periodicals   **39**

Indexes to Scholarly and Professional Journals   **46**
Locating Periodicals   **47**
Additional Resources   **48**
Some General Bibliographies, Periodical Indexes, and
    Representative Journals   **50**
Review Questions   **55**
Exercises   **55**

4   **SEARCHING FOR SOURCES**   **57**

Compiling the Working Bibliography   **57**
Gathering Your Sources   **59**
Reassessing Your Topic   **61**
Skimming Your Sources   **63**
Evaluating Potential Sources   **65**
Review Questions   **70**
Exercises   **70**

5   **READING THE SOURCES AND TAKING NOTES   72**

Practical Aspects of Note-taking   **72**
The Fine Art of Note-taking   **75**
Paraphrasing   **76**
Summarizing   **77**
Quoting   **79**
An Extended Example of Effective Note-taking   **86**
The Problem of Plagiarism   **97**
Review Questions   **101**
Exercises   **102**

6   **PREPARING TO WRITE THE PAPER**   **107**

Sorting Your Note Cards   **107**
Asking Yourself Questions to Determine Your
    Thesis   **108**
The Introductory Paragraph   **110**
Outlining   **112**
Review Questions   **118**
Exercise   **118**

7   **WRITING THE PAPER**   **120**

Writing the Rough Draft   **120**
Revising the Rough Draft   **123**
Writing the Polished, Final Draft   **130**
Review Questions   **130**
Exercise   **130**

8   **DOCUMENTING YOUR SOURCES**   **131**

What to Document   **132**
Basic Information Provided by Documentation   **134**
The Bibliography   **135**
Common Bibliographic Forms   **135**
Some Less Common Bibliographic Forms   **138**
Footnotes and Endnotes   **142**
Basic Forms for Endnotes   **142**
Less Common Note Forms   **144**
Footnote Format   **147**
Documentation of Illustrative Materials   **149**
Other Forms of Documentation   **150**
Forms for Lists of References in Disciplines Outside the
    Humanities   **153**
Review Questions   **156**
Exercise   **157**

9   **PREPARING THE FINAL MANUSCRIPT**   **159**

The Mechanics of Manuscript Preparation   **159**
Two Sample Research Papers
    "Jefferson Davis as President: A Confederate
    Asset"   **162**
    "Emily Dickinson's Reluctance to Publish"   **179**

Preface

The library research paper can be a freshman English student's most exciting and liberating assignment. It is also, of course, the most demanding. Ideally, the student chooses a research topic that is both significant and workable, conceives a realistic plan for executing the project, and compiles a broad yet selective list of available sources. The student then extracts information and ideas from these sources through critical reading and composes a confident and enlightening essay.

That's asking a great deal, of course, and we have found that students need considerable help at every stage. Yet most books on the research paper—even those intended, like ours, specifically for freshmen—seem to presuppose readers who are already comfortable with the techniques of planning, writing, and revising and whose main requirement is advice on matters of form. In our book, although we treat formal matters fully, our main concern is to explain the *process* of producing a research paper, with particular attention to the steps that give students the most trouble.

The first such steps involve planning. Every experienced researcher knows that the success or failure of a research project often depends on the first choice made: that of a topic. The risk of a mistake is especially great when the researcher is a beginner, with only a sketchy knowledge of the field in which he or she is working. For this reason we offer more advice and problem-solving examples than most other texts do, showing students how to inform themselves well enough to choose practical topics. We also demonstrate how to use a tentative thesis, or hypothesis, as a tool for evaluating potential sources and guiding research. The earlier the student can determine what she or he is looking for, the more focused and efficient the process becomes. And even if the hypothesis or topic is subsequently changed, the benefits from these preliminary steps are not entirely lost.

Getting from a stack of note cards to a rough draft is another especially troublesome stage in the process, and we devote two chapters to it. Chapter 6 discusses the assimilation of the research notes, with an emphasis on outlining and on composing an introductory paragraph. Chapter 7 is a guide to writing the draft, using the introductory paragraph as a springboard and the outline as a means of keeping the draft under control. This chapter also includes detailed advice on revising paragraphs, sentences, and word choice.

Finally, Chapter 8 offers a thorough discussion of documentation, beginning with the MLA style but also showing sample notes and bibliographic entries in the styles used by other disciplines in the humanities, natural sciences, and social sciences. Chapters 2 through 8, the core of the book, include questions to help students review the concepts introduced and exercises to give students practice in applying those concepts.

Throughout the book—as we explore the sequence of activities and decisions that make up the process of planning, researching, writing, and documenting the paper—we follow the progress of two students as they work through the process themselves: choose topics, formulate (and reformulate) hypotheses, gather and evaluate sources, read the sources and take notes, organize and write their drafts, and prepare their final manuscripts. Both their papers, one historical and the other literary, are reproduced in full in Chapter 9.

From the beginning of our work on this book we have benefited from thoughtful, constructive advice, and now we can express our gratitude in public. Our colleague Lewis Schwartz was especially helpful during the crucial early stages, and we also want to thank Lynn Z. Bloom, Linda Coleman, Joseph Comprone, Elizabeth Cowan, Robert Farrell, Richard Gebhart, Laurie Kirszner, Shirley Morahan, Duncan Rollo, Alfred Rosa, Leonard Vogt, and Suzanne Wolkenfeld for their help along the way. We also want to show our appreciation to the editors at St. Martin's Press, especially to Peter Phelps, who convinced us of the need for this book and guided it through its initial stages; to Tom Broadbent and Nancy Perry for their optimistic appraisals of the work in progress; to John Francis, who kept our concept firmly in mind while rendering invaluable critical aid and editorial assistance; and to Charles Thurlow and Marcia Muth for their conscientious copyediting and skillful preparation of the final manuscript for publication.

Stephen Weidenborner
Domenick Caruso

1
An Introduction to the Process

As you think about writing a research paper, you may wonder how this assignment differs from other papers you have written. The basic difference is that most of the ideas that go into a research paper come from materials found in a library. The paper does not grow out of your personal experiences and opinions as some other compositions do.

Sometimes virtually all of the information and ideas that appear in a research paper will come from books, magazine articles, and other sources. Your contribution consists mainly of finding the information and presenting it in a coherent essay. At other times, you will be encouraged to add your own judgments to the ideas you have gathered from various sources. Either assignment may be referred to as a *term paper* or a *research paper,* and both demand that you know how to do research as well as how to put together a good essay.

You should recognize at the start that producing a good research paper involves a great deal of work. On the broadest level, you must complete the following steps:

- make sure that your chosen topic is workable,
- find sources (usually books and articles in magazines, newspapers, and scholarly journals) that provide information specifically related to the topic,

- examine these materials closely and record all relevant information in detailed notes, and
- organize your research findings in a substantial essay (usually seven to ten pages in length).

To accomplish all this, and to do the job well, you should allow several weeks. Your first research paper may well require a month or more of your time as you learn to master an unfamiliar process.

Although writing a research paper is more complicated than writing an essay based on personal experience or your own ideas, the rewards of this work are great. As you increase your knowledge about a topic and begin making judgments as to which information is relevant to your purpose and which writers' interpretations are valid, you will rapidly become an expert on your topic—someone who really knows and whose opinions therefore carry some weight.

Some Essential Definitions

Before we look into the specific activities that make up the research process, we need to introduce some basic research terms. Although some of these terms may seem familiar because they are often applied to the writing of essays in general, be sure to note their specific applications to writing research papers.

- **Subject**—a broad area of study, such as *adolescent behavior, modern European politics, Shakespeare's tragedies,* or *prehistoric animals,* which can be narrowed down to **topics** suitable for research papers.
- **Topic**—a relatively narrow area of study that can be thoroughly investigated within the limits of a given research assignment. Some reasonably narrow topics might be *how parental attitudes affect teenage alcoholism, the effects of terrorism on the social policies of the Italian government, the relationships between young women and their fathers in several Shakespearean tragedies, the possible role of humans in the extinction of large prehistoric North American mammals.*
- **Hypothesis**—a prediction, made before reading the sources closely, of what you expect your *thesis* (see below) will be. This "educated guess" guides your search for information by focusing your attention on specific aspects of your topic.
- **Thesis**—a general statement, placed in the introduction to your paper, which announces to your readers the major conclusions uncovered through your research. The main body of your paper explains, illustrates, argues for, or, in some sense, proves the thesis.

A good way to see what a research paper does is to read one or two of them. You will find two in chapter 9.

An Outline of the Research Process

Now that you have some idea of what a good research paper looks like, we can begin examining the research process in more detail. As the following outline shows, the research assignment consists of three fairly distinct kinds of work—research itself, analytical reading, and writing—all of which require good judgment, language skill, and hard work. The fourth phase concerns formal matters, which are also important to the final product.

PHASE ONE: PRELIMINARY RESEARCH

STEP ONE:
Defining Your Objective

Choose an interesting *subject*, if the choice is left to you. Narrow the subject to a *topic* that can be thoroughly researched within the assigned limits of the paper. This can be accomplished by brainstorming and by reading about the subject in general reference works. After selecting a topic, you should form a reasonable *hypothesis*.

STEP TWO:
Finding Sources

Go to the library, and put together a working bibliography, a list of sources that seem to be directly related to your topic. Reconsider your choice of topic if you cannot find enough sources or if you find so many potential sources that your topic is probably too broad for your assignment. Skim through these sources to see whether your hypothesis still seems reasonable. Be ready to revise the hypothesis to conform to what your skimming reveals.

PHASE TWO: READING

STEP THREE:
Reading and Taking Notes

Once you have a reasonable hypothesis and a sufficient number of sources, begin reading the sources closely and taking detailed notes that record all information directly related to your hypothesis.

STEP FOUR:
Arriving at a Thesis

Analyze the information in your notes in order to decide whether your hypothesis is accurate. If so, it can become the thesis for your paper. If the hypothesis is not fully supported, revise it to reflect your findings accurately. State your thesis in an introductory paragraph, and organize your note cards in order to produce an outline for your paper.

PHASE THREE: WRITING

STEP FIVE:
Writing the Paper

Write a full paper in three drafts: a rough version in which you concentrate on the flow of thought; a first revision in which you check and revise the organization, if necessary, and improve the style; and a second revision in which you eliminate formal errors.

PHASE FOUR: FINISHING UP

STEP SIX:
Documenting Your
Sources

Prepare a bibliography (or reference list) that lists all the sources that contributed to your paper. Also add footnotes (or endnotes) to identify each source as it is used in the paper.

STEP SEVEN:
Preparing the Final
Manuscript

Type a manuscript of the paper, following the format shown in this book or one that your instructor has approved. Make at least one copy for yourself, to insure against accidental loss, and submit the original copy to the instructor.

A glance at this research outline might lead you to believe that you can arrive at a thesis by following a simple, step-by-step prescription—moving from *subject* to *topic* to *hypothesis* to *thesis*. In actual practice, however, you must be ready at every step to revise decisions made earlier, as your research produces additional information. This is especially true for the hypothesis which, after all, is only a prediction of what you will discover. So, although this book must present the research process as a straightforward series of evolving steps, you should remember that you may have to rethink earlier work every now and then.

2

Defining Your Objective

At the heart of every successful research paper lies a strong thesis, which the writer explains, illustrates, argues for, or in some sense proves by organizing in a coherent essay the evidence he or she has gathered from various sources. And, as you will see, finding sources and extracting useful information from them will be much easier if you start with a hypothesis, or reasonable guess as to what your research will uncover. The more you know about a topic, the easier it is to think of a hypothesis that predicts fairly closely what your thesis will be. But in some courses, you will have to deal with relatively unfamiliar topics which may make it difficult to think of a good hypothesis. At such times, you will want to have an orderly procedure for coming up with a reasonable hypothesis. This chapter describes such a procedure.

Choosing a Subject

The first phase of writing a research paper involves defining the question the paper will answer—the problem your research will explore and try to solve. Your first thoughts may be very general: "I want to write about Middle Eastern politics;" "I want to write about dinosaurs;" "I want to write about Roman Catholicism;" "I want to write about Emily Dickinson;" "I want to write about the Civil War." You don't yet know what you want to say about any of these subjects, or even whether you can find a good research project in any of them, but in choosing a subject like *Middle Eastern politics* or *Emily Dickinson,* you have already made your first important decision, the one on which all your other decisions will depend.

What makes a good subject for a research paper? First of all, the subject should be in a field you already know something about. Your object in doing research is to become enough of an expert to write with some authority, and it is much harder to become an expert from scratch than to build on what you already know. Second, you should be strongly interested in your subject and really want to learn more about it. Doing a research paper requires much time and concentrated effort, and the project will be an unpleasant chore if you don't care about your subject. Finally, your subject should raise some questions that call for research in the library.

As you saw in the outline of the research process, choosing a subject is only the first of several decisions you make during your preliminary research. Next, within your subject, you must find a topic, a specific problem you will attempt to solve. Identifying a good topic requires time and thought, so you should choose your subject as early in the term as possible. Do not wait for the instructor to announce the due date and other details. Once you have a subject, you can be on the alert for possible topics while doing your reading for the course and listening to lectures and class discussions.

Choosing a Topic

Moving from a general subject to a specific topic is what this chapter is about. This phase of the research process should not be done carelessly because the success of your project depends on your choice of topic. Many writers make the mistake of rushing right to the library, getting a stack of books off the shelves, and taking piles of notes before they have fully defined a problem. Then, after days or even weeks of work, they find they have no control over the project, no sense of its direction, and no time to go back and begin again.

The topic you choose to study and write about should be an aspect of your subject which is neither so broad that your research will uncover far more information than you can possibly use nor so narrow that just one or two sources will cover all that is known about it. Your topic should be a problem that has not been decisively solved, a question on which your research may shed some light. There is not much to say, for example, about why the sky is blue; that question has long since been answered. So have many seemingly more complex questions, such as "How does the ozone layer in the upper atmosphere protect the earth from cosmic rays?" You will be able to find many sources that discuss this topic, but all of them will say much the same thing because a single explanation is accepted as fact by the experts. Your research into this topic would be very easy: all you would have to do is restate in your own words what you had read in any one of the many available sources. Serious research projects must tackle greater challenges than that!

Many suitable topics can be derived from a single subject. For example, students interested in the same subject, *the work of Leonardo da Vinci,* might select topics as diverse as *his knowledge of human anatomy, his designs for war machines,* or *his tendency to leave his works unfinished.* As suggested earlier, one way of exploring various topics is through your class work. Here are two other techniques for developing topics.

BRAINSTORMING

One way to get ideas for research topics is by brainstorming, a widely used technique for creating ideas and putting them into some permanent form. You can brainstorm with other people or by yourself, and you can record your ideas any way you like—the easiest way is with a tape recorder, but you can also write them down. Here are a few simple guidelines:

1. *Ask yourself questions.* You are looking for a question suitable for research. When you are brainstorming, ask yourself many, many questions about your subject.

2. *Don't censor yourself.* Record every question you think of, even if it does not seem relevant at the moment. Your purpose in brainstorming is to have lots of ideas to choose from. Later you can decide which are good, but evaluating them now will slow down or stop the flow of questions.

3. *Set a time limit.* If you use a tape recorder, limit yourself to ten or fifteen minutes; if you are writing your ideas down, allow twenty minutes or so. These limits are long enough to give you time for ideas, yet short enough to help you concentrate.

4. *Take a break.* Don't try to select a topic as soon as you stop recording your ideas. Put your notes aside for an hour or so. You will return to them refreshed and better able to make decisions. (Of course, if you come up with more ideas in the meantime, you can add them to the products of your brainstorming.)

Here is the result of ten minutes of brainstorming about dinosaurs:

What *is* a dinosaur, anyway? Where did dinosaurs live? What did they eat? Did any other creatures eat them? How long did it take them to evolve from earlier life forms? How long did they survive on earth? Are crocodiles modern dinosaurs? Are birds descended from dinosaurs? How smart were they? Were any humans around at the time they became extinct? Why did they become extinct? Because of their size? Because they weren't able to compete with smarter creatures that came along later? Because the weather changed all over the world? Because of some natural catastrophe? Could some dinosaurs still exist today, living in some remote section of Africa or South America or on an unexplored island? Where are fossil dinosaurs being found today? When were these fossils first discovered? Are the bones found all in one place so we can see just what a real dinosaur looked like? Or must the bones be assembled according to a scientist's idea of what the living dinosaurs looked like?

In this example, several themes can be discerned: *the reason for extinction, the possibility that extinction was not total* (some living species may be modern dinosaurs, or some dinosaurs may have survived in isolation), and *the extent of our knowledge about these creatures.* Any of these themes might serve as a reasonable topic for investigation, but this cannot be certain until the next step in the research process.

BACKGROUND READING

Once you think you have a good topic, you should next go to the library to do some background reading in your subject area. This work consists of looking up your subject in general reference works—encyclopedias, biographical dictionaries, and books that survey broad areas such as modern art, ancient Greece, Western philosophy, Romantic literature, abnormal psychology, or the history of astronomy. Most of these materials are located in the reference room. Since such items are constantly being used by many people, they cannot be removed from the room. You should therefore be prepared to do all your preliminary research in the library. A list of some widely available general reference books appears at the end of this chapter. The reference librarian can tell you about others if you need them.

The purposes behind background reading are first to become more familiar with your subject as a whole and second to discover the best available topic or to confirm the strength of your topic choice. Even when you are convinced your topic is sound, do not skip this step or cut it short. By strengthening your grasp of the subject area as a whole, you will be in a better position to understand the wealth of ideas and information that you will be sifting through when working with your sources.

When doing preliminary research, you will find it useful to take notes that you can refer to later if you need to revise your original topic and hypothesis. In taking these notes, avoid recording detailed factual information. Concentrate instead on gaining a clear overview of the subject. Make sure that the broad picture is not buried by a flood of facts.

Do not read entire books during preliminary research. Look for short articles or chapters in general reference works. For instance, if your subject is *Martin Luther King, Jr.*, do not begin by reading a full-length biography of the man. Since you do not yet have a definite topic, most of the book will not be directly relevant to whatever topic you eventually select. But even if you have a definite topic in mind, such as *King's relationships with the most militant black leaders,* you would do well to review King's career as a civil rights advocate in an encyclopedia or a biographical dictionary where you would find a concise account of the major events in his life.

TWO STUDENTS FIND THEIR TOPICS

You have already read the two sample freshman research papers in Chapter 9 of this book. Obviously those papers did not just appear out of the blue. Each student worked hard and systematically to choose a topic, gather information, and use that information to solve the problem posed by the topic.

George Pitman had long been interested in the Civil War and, more specifically, in Jefferson Davis, the only president of the Confederate States of America. On the day the research paper was assigned, he knew he wanted to study *Jefferson Davis*. Since he realized that this topic was far too broad and could fill an entire book, he submitted a more limited topic, *Jefferson Davis's public life.* Even though this topic would exclude many parts of Davis's life, such as his childhood, his education, his family life, and his work in private business, the student and his instructor agreed that it was still too broad since Davis had also served as an officer in the Mexican War and as a United States senator before becoming president of the Confederacy. To cover so much within seven to ten pages would be impossible.

In addition, they discussed the basic defect of the topic *Jefferson Davis's public life*—that it was not a topic at all because, as a simply factual account, it suggested no questions for investigation. The instructor advised the student to find a topic that posed some controversial question about Davis about which the experts, in this case Civil War historians, disagreed, and that was narrow enough so that the paper would not be superficial. The student then began his background reading with the entries for "Civil War" and "Jefferson Davis" in a general encyclopedia, in this case the *Encyclopedia Americana*.

Here is the "Jefferson Davis" entry, reproduced in full. Several fairly narrow possible topics are suggested by the headings within the article—**Service as Senator, Secretary of War, President of the Confederacy,** and **Fighting the Civil War.** Each identifies a potential area of investigation and evaluation. The student's keen interest in the war itself led him to focus on the last two sections. He particularly noted the mixed judgments of Davis's performance as president and therefore decided on the topic *Davis's performance as president of the Confederacy.*

Beside the Davis entry are some marginal comments illustrating how the student analyzed the information in the article to find a topic for research.

Student spots a possible topic in Davis's being "personally blamed" for the South's failure but later admired for his "devotion to the Southern cause."

Student notes the possibility of comparing or contrasting Davis and Lincoln but suspects that this topic might be too big. Student wonders if this topic could be narrowed to a specific point of comparison or contrast. He notes Davis's sensitivity to criticism as a possible area for research.

Student finds this general biographical information too noncontroversial for a research topic, but he notes Davis's early interest in military affairs.

DAVIS, Jefferson (1808– 1889), American political leader, who was president of the Confederate States of America during the four years of its existence (1861– 1865). A senator and for a time secretary of war (1853– 1857) in the United States government but a spokesman for the South, he reluctantly abandoned the Union during the secessionist movement. As president of the Confederacy, he led the South in the Civil War and was personally blamed for its failures. After the Confederate defeat, however, he was widely admired in the South for his unrelenting devotion to the Southern cause.

Over six feet tall, strong-jawed and hollow-cheeked, his body worn thin by work, worry, and disease, Davis was blind in one eye, had an acutely sensitive nervous system, and suffered from neuralgia. In contrast to Abraham Lincoln, he was graceful and highly educated, but, though he pushed himself unmercifully, he could not approach Lincoln's simplicity, sincere eloquence, humanity, and insight into fundamental problems. Criticism stung Davis deeply, and lacking Lincoln's singleness of purpose, he was unable to dismiss detractors and concentrate on his goals.

Early Life. Davis was born in Christian (now Todd) county, Ky., on June 3, 1808, the youngest of 10 children of Samuel and Jane Cook Davis, who were respectively of Welsh and Scotch-Irish heritage. A few years after his birth the family settled in the new but prosperous cotton region of Wilkinson county, Miss.

Because the frontier schools were inadequate, young Jefferson studied for a few years at a Dominican school in Kentucky and then returned home and attended nearby private academies. At the age of 13 he entered Transylvania College in Kentucky, and he had completed his junior year there when his already prominent oldest brother, Joseph, secured his appointment to West Point in 1824. Jefferson's record at the Military Academy was not distinguished; he was graduated 23d in a class of 33, and his drinking in a public tavern and other escapades brought more than the average number of demerits. However, he developed an abiding interest in military affairs, philosophy, and history.

After graduation in 1828, Davis served as a lieutenant on the northwestern frontier. There he met and fell in love with Sarah Knox, daughter of his commander, Col. Zachary Taylor. But Jefferson's attentions to an Indian girl at a dance and his opposition to Taylor's policies angered the colonel, and the marriage was delayed. The Black Hawk War (1832) gave Davis some military experience, but in 1835, having secured Taylor's reluctant consent, he resigned his commission to marry Sarah Knox. The young couple settled on a 1,000-acre (400-hectare) cotton plantation in the Mississippi delta given them by Joseph, but less than three months after the wedding Sarah Knox was dead of malaria.

Davis found release in developing the plantation, which was known as Brierfield. A beneficent master to his own slaves, he always saw slavery in its most ideal light, holding himself accountable both for the well-being of his slaves and for their training in responsibility. Yet he believed that God created Negroes inferior to whites, and that neither education nor environment could counteract the divine intent. Rather than seeing the conflict between Christianity and human bondage, Davis found justification in the Old Testament for slavery. The profits from Brierfield and the relative contentment of his slaves supported his convictions.

Political Beginnings. By 1843, Davis' reputation as a scholar together with the tradition of planter participation in politics, won him a last-minute Democratic nomination for the Mississippi legislature. His brief but intensive campaign gained an impressive, though not victorious, vote in a strong Whig county. He broke with his party's stand on repudiation of the Union Bank bonds, but political enemies later repeatedly and falsely accused him of being a repudiator. Campaigning for James Polk in 1844 and advocating territorial expansion, he canvassed the state and proved himself a popular orator.

The following year Davis married Varina Howell, a member of the local Mississippi aristocracy. He received the Democratic nomination for the House of Representatives and won election by advocating sound currency, a low tariff, and territorial expansion. In Congress he joined forces on the question of expansion with Southerners who urged moderation and compromise rather than war with Britain. But his stay in the House was short, for he resigned in 1846 to command the Mississippi Rifles in the Mexican War.

At the Battle of Monterrey, Colonel Davis won respect for his personal bravery; at Buena Vista, he demonstrated both courage and ability, but was wounded and

wonders if this
information connects
with Davis's early
interest in military
affairs.

Student notes
Davis's change from
nationalist to
sectionalist.

Student notes
Davis's concept of
the sovereignty of
states under the
Constitution as a
possible topic.

Student reads this
background
information but takes
no notes.

Student notes
Davis's return to
national rather than
sectional interests.
Student also adds a
note about Davis as
secretary of war to
his previous ones on

returned home. Now a hero, his political career was advanced.

Service as Senator. In 1847, Davis was appointed by the governor of Mississippi to a vacancy in the U.S. Senate, and the next year the state legislature elected him for the remainder of the unexpired term. As a member of the Committee on Military Affairs he supported expansion and enlarging the army. Already the young Mississippi senator foresaw a transcontinental railroad and a Panama railway to promote commerce and secure Pacific coast defenses.

Yet, little by little, Davis became more a sectionalist and less a nationalist. The Wilmot Proviso and the Compromise of 1850 (qq.v.) turned his energies toward the defense of slavery. He envisioned no relief in Calhoun's discredited doctrine of nullification, but held that the Union was composed of sovereign independent states, voluntarily confederated and free to resume their sovereignty. Thus secession was not revolution but a legal remedy. Davis favored preservation of the Union, if the Constitution remained "in the form and with the meaning it had when it left the hands of its authors." The federal government should respect the right of property in slaves; any interference with it was unconstitutional and a threat to state sovereignty. Davis voiced his convictions well and was an excellent debater, but in his constitutional theories he closed his eyes to custom and practice that had already brought a changed interpretation of the Constitution to a majority of Americans. He opposed the Compromise of 1850, contending that a strict fugitive slave law could not be enforced in face of adverse public opinion, that the states alone could exclude slavery from the territories, and that the Missouri Compromise line should be extended to the Pacific.

After passage of the Compromise of 1850, Davis signed a vigorous protest and, notwithstanding his recent election to a six-year term in the Senate, resigned (1851) to accept the Democratic nomination for governor of Mississippi. He waged a strong campaign, but lost to Henry S. Foote. Discredited and dismayed, Davis returned to his plantation until his interest in Franklin Pierce's presidential candidacy brought him back to politics. After his election, Pierce urged Davis to accept a cabinet position.

Secretary of War. Davis reached the apex of his national career as secretary of war. In his direction of the War Department he was more a nationalist than a sectionalist. He revised military regulations, replaced wood gun carriages with iron, adopted a better system of infantry tactics, provided rifles, pistols, and the Minié ball, used large-grain powder, and created the medical service. The Military Academy was enlarged, four regiments

Davis's interest in military affairs. This topic, however, still does not seem to go beyond an accumulation of facts, so the student doubts it will be a good topic.

Student adds to previous note on Davis's attitude toward slavery.

Student takes more notes on Davis's belief in the sovereignty of states but realizes that these notes are much like his previous ones on the point. Student suspects that further research in this area may uncover only repetitious material.

Student takes notes on Davis as a "cooperative secessionist" and considers how this relates to his other

were added to the army, and coastal and frontier defenses were strengthened. These reforms, plus increased pay, endeared Davis to the military, but he failed in the attempt to make merit rather than seniority the basis for promotion. His introduction of camels for transportation in the West was interesting but ineffectual.

As secretary he had charge of enlarging the Capitol building and constructing a viaduct that provided a better water system for Washington. Undoubtedly his greatest contribution was the survey of routes for western railways and the resulting detailed reports, which not only laid the basis for future railroads but also emphasized the importance of the great West. Though a strict constructionist, Davis advocated federal land grants and bonds to encourage railroad construction, on the ground that transcontinental routes were necessary for national defense and thus within the war powers of the president. Davis favored the Southern route to the West and was instrumental in securing the Gadsden Purchase from Mexico. He favored the acquisition of Cuba and territorial rights in Nicaragua.

Return to the Senate. On the expiration of his term as secretary in 1857, Davis was elected to the Senate. He returned to that body as the recognized spokesman of the South, proclaiming slavery an economic and moral good and openly supporting its extension. At the same time he evidenced a sincere love of the Union and an unwillingness to see it broken by radical Northern or Southern action.

Representing the Southern wing of the Democratic party, on Feb. 2, 1860, Davis introduced resolutions that became the platform of most Southern men. In them he reiterated his position that the federal Constitution was adopted by free and independent sovereign states and protested that Negro slavery was recognized as legitimate and that attacks on it were manifest breaches of good faith. He further declared that neither Congress nor a territorial legislature could impair the right of a citizen to move freely with his property in the territories and that therefore it was the duty of Congress to provide adequate protection for slave property. This doctrine of congressional protection of slavery in territories was accepted as the minority platform at the Charleston Democratic Convention; upon adoption of the majority report supported by Stephen A. Douglas, eight Southern states left the convention.

Davis eventually favored John C. Breckinridge in the presidential campaign of 1860, and after the election of Abraham Lincoln, he was no more than a cooperative secessionist. He held that the Southern states should meet to determine a new policy and repeatedly warned that there could be no peaceful secession. Davis served

notes on Davis's
choices between
sectional and
national interests.

Student notes
Davis's relationships
with other
Confederate leaders
as a possible topic.

Student sees a
possible topic
dealing with Davis's
success as president
of the Confederacy.

on the Senate Committee of Thirteen and favored the Crittenden Compromise (q.v.), but, seeing no prospects for effective compromise, he voted against it. On Jan 5, 1861, he joined other Southern senators in urging each state to secede as soon as possible and to provide the means of organizing a Southern Confederacy. Yet even at this late date he realized the danger in leaving the Union and saw advantage to the South in keeping Southern senators and representatives in Congress.

After Mississippi seceded, Davis resigned and returned home, where he accepted the rank of major general and the command of his state's military forces before he was informed of his selection by the Provisional Congress as president of the Confederacy. Reluctantly he left for Montgomery, Ala., and the impossible task ahead, for he would have preferred an army command.

President of the Confederacy. Davis took office as president of the Confederacy on Feb. 18, 1861. He selected his cabinet with due regard to geography, personality, political connection, and ability. In Judah P. Benjamin, first attorney general, then secretary of war, and finally secretary of state; Stephen R. Mallory, secretary of the navy; and John H. Reagan, postmaster general, he found men of outstanding ability who remained with him throughout the Confederacy. Christopher G. Memminger and George A. Trenholm as secretaries of the treasury directed the department well—considering the financial deficiencies of the South. Eleven other men served in the cabinet, and most of them resigned because of personal ambition or congressional opposition.

Though confident that law and right were on his side, President Davis was equally convinced that the major force was on the other. Behind him he had little more than 9 million people, including slaves, and woefully inadequate industrial facilities in contrast to the North's population of 22 million, extensive industry, and almost unlimited possibilities for men and matériel. The South did, however, have certain advantages, including a citizenry accustomed to outdoor life and trained in the use of firearms, excellent military officers, a defensive position, and slaves who remained loyal and economically productive.

Davis pressed military preparation, but planned no overt act to give the North cause for war. Though anxious to avoid a test of strength, the course of events forced him to consent to the bombardment of Fort Sumter, S.C. (April 12–13, 1861), which gave Lincoln the opportunity to accuse the South of aggression.

Fighting the Civil War. Davis and his cabinet used Southern resources well. Approximately 900,000 men volunteered or were conscripted for the army: ordnance and munition works were constructed so rapidly that no Southern army really suffered a lack of these supplies; a poor transportation system was improved: and scrap iron and captured steam engines were converted into a modern navy, whose ironclad ships and torpedoes lessened the effectiveness of the Northern blockade, thereby enabling the South to obtain essential supplies by blockade runners from abroad. Confederate cruisers roamed the seas, effectively destroying the Union's carrying trade.

Student notes the problems Davis faced as president for possible research.

Excess cotton and the failure of England and France to demand it at the possible cost of war created a problem, because the blockade limited cotton's expected value as a source of exchange and made it impossible for the debtor South to finance an extended war. Yet cotton became the medium of exchange for matériel secured by blockade-running.

Southern opposition to heavy taxation, together with an inability to buy bonds, forced the financing of war with fiat money. The resulting depreciation of the currency created a morale problem and made necessary taxation in kind and impressment of commodities at fixed prices.

In foreign affairs Davis and Benjamin pushed every conceivable advantage, but for many reasons, including its critical need of Northern wheat, Britain refused recognition, and France feared to act alone.

Student notes criticisms of Davis's leadership and recalls his earlier note about Davis being blamed and then admired. Student notes the judgments about Davis's leadership as well as controversial decisions made by Davis.

From first to last, severe criticism fell on Davis. His accusers blamed him for the inadequacies of the South, charged him with being a dictator, condemned him for interfering with military commanders, criticized his appointments, and demanded an offensive rather than a defensive military policy.

With few exceptions, including his blind faith in Braxton Bragg and the removal of Joseph E. Johnston, Davis selected his officers intelligently; and the army of Robert E. Lee, which he visited and with which he interfered most often, had more successes than any other. Perhaps his greatest mistake lay in overemphasis on the defense of Richmond, Va., and failure to recognize the importance of the West. He probed the relative merits of East and West in 1863 and eventually supported Lee's planned invasion rather than the reinforcement of Vicksburg, Miss.

Student notes the problems Davis confronted as president and starts thinking that a paper evaluating Davis's performance as president might prove interesting.

The degree of congressional opposition was indicated by Davis' 39 veto messages, and, although the Congress could not override these vetoes, by 1865 the President had lost the confidence of Congress and the public. Opposition of Georgia's and North Carolina's governors, widespread desertions, and capture of the last port of entry, forced approval of arming Negroes. But before this became reality, the Confederacy fell.

In Defeat. On April 3, 1865, Davis and his cabinet fled Richmond (stopping briefly in Danville, Va., and Greensboro, N.C.) and at Charlotte, N.C., operated as a government for the last time. Davis sped through South Carolina and into Georgia. Ostensibly headed for the trans-Mississippi region and continued resistance, he actually loitered in Georgia awaiting capture, knowing that the Confederacy was at an end.

On May 10 he was taken at Irwinville, Ga. Accused of treason and of participation in planning the assassination of Lincoln, he was imprisoned at Fortress Monroe, Va. For a time he wore leg shackles and this, with other harsh treatment, restored his popularity in the South and made him, second to Lee, a symbol of the Confederacy. Though twice indicted, he was never brought to trial, and in two years (on May 13, 1867) he was released. That only Capt. Henry Wirz, commandant of Andersonville prison, was executed as a result of so long and bloody a war is remarkable in the annals of history.

The Remaining Years. For the rest of his long life, Davis was a defender and apologist of the South. Failure of several business ventures left him in straitened financial circumstances, which the gift of the Beauvoir plantation at Biloxi, Miss., partially eased. There he collected material for his *The Rise and Fall of the Confederate Government* (1881) and wrote an excellent exposition of the Southern point of view and a justification of secession. Yet, much of his writing was special pleading rather than history and was disappointing in its meager revelations of intimate associations during the war years. Davis accepted few of the numerous invitations for speeches; but, whenever he spoke, he stressed the right of secession, the justice of the Confederate cause, and on occasion disparaged the federal government. Acrimonious controversies with former Confederates such as Gen. Joseph E. Johnston and Northerners such as Gen. William T. Sherman clouded his declining years, but in 1886 he received triumphal ovations after appearances in Montgomery, Ala., Atlanta, Ga., and Savannah, Ga.

Although he remained the sharp-tongued defender of the Confederacy, Davis apparently had mellowed by his 80th year. He never requested or received a pardon, yet stated in a speech at Mississippi City, Miss.: "The past is dead; let it bury its dead, its hopes, and its aspirations; before you lies the future—a future full of golden promise, a future of expanding national glory, before which all the world shall stand amazed." In November 1889, while visiting Brierfield, he became ill and returned as far as New Orleans, La., where he died on December 6.

See also CIVIL WAR; CONFEDERATE STATES OF AMERICA.

REMBERT W. PATRICK
Author of "Jefferson Davis and His Cabinet"

Student takes notes on Davis's influence after the Civil War.

After the student finishes the article, he reviews the possible topics he has noted about Davis—his interest in military affairs, his attitude toward slavery, his change from nationalist to sectionalist, his concept of the sovereignty of states, his relationships with other Confederate leaders, and his influence after the Civil War. Student decides that Davis's performance as president is his most promising topic since it combines his original interest in the Civil War period with a clear issue about Davis.

The student now turns to the "Civil War" entry in search of additional information about this topic after noting for the future the other sources of information listed here. (This list will give the student a head start when he begins searching for sources.)

Bibliography

Davis, Jefferson, *The Rise and Fall of the Confederate Government*, 2 vols. (New York 1881).

Davis, Varina H., *Jefferson Davis, Ex-President of the Confederate States of America: A Memoir,* 2 vols. (New York 1890).

Dodd, William E., *Life of Jefferson Davis* (Philadelphia 1907; repr. New York 1965).

McElroy, Robert McN. *Jefferson Davis, the Real and the Unreal,* 2 vols. (New York 1937).

Patrick, Rembert W., *Jefferson Davis and His Cabinet* (Baton Rouge, La., 1944).

Strode, Hudson, *Jefferson Davis,* 3 vols. (New York 1955–1964).

Strode, Hudson, ed., *Jefferson Davis: Private Letters, 1823–1899* (New York 1966).

Vandiver, Frank E., *Jefferson Davis and the Confederate State* (New York 1964).

Susanna Andrews arrived at her topic more easily. She was taking a course in modern poetry and early in the semester had been reading poems by Emily Dickinson in her textbook. Excited by the poetry, she was also struck by a remark in the book's introduction to Dickinson: "She did not write for publication and was easily discouraged from it; only eight of her nearly 1800 poems were published during her lifetime." Later, when she read about Dickinson in a general reference book, *The Oxford Companion to American Literature,* she found a statement to the effect that only six of the poet's poems had been published during her life, and those without her consent; even Dickinson's family had not been allowed to read her poetry. The student wanted to know why Dickinson had published so little of her poetry. Her instructor told her that the problem had not been decisively solved, so she confidently chose as her topic *Emily Dickinson's reluctance to publish her poems.*

As these two examples show, finding a topic during preliminary research is not always a simple process. Potentially good topics do not stand out from the pages in boldface type, though, as you have seen, headings in the text can be helpful. A good guideline is to look for issues on which the experts differ or for significant, unexplained, and questionable "facts." Even if it is not possible to find a decisive solution to the problem you choose to investigate, locating and presenting the arguments and evidence on the various sides can produce a worthwhile research paper.

Forming a Hypothesis

So far we have discussed the choice of topic as though you had to make this decision before moving on to the next task of your preliminary research, forming a hypothesis about your topic. In fact, the hypothesis may occur to you at the same time you choose your topic. This is only natural when you consider that the topic embodies an unanswered question, and the hypothesis is a tentative answer.

The key to producing a successful research paper is the ability to arrive at a reasonable hypothesis as early as possible. When you read your sources in search of useful information, you will often find that the topic alone does not provide sharp enough focus. You will come across a great deal of information that touches on your topic in one way or another, but as a whole, such pieces of information will not hang together well. Your notes will look like a "grocery list" of loosely related ideas and facts. A paper consisting only of such materials would lack focus and do little more than show that you had spent a good many hours in the library.

To prevent this from happening, you can look ahead to the writing phase when you will need a thesis, just as you do for most other compositions. The thesis will state the major conclusions of your research, and the main body of the paper will demonstrate or, in some sense, prove that statement.

You might wish that you could know your thesis from the beginning so that you could limit your reading in each source to those pages that support or oppose the thesis. Of course, you cannot know in advance what results will come out of your research—what your thesis will be. But you can begin work by thinking about the topic in terms of a possible thesis, or hypothesis. This hypothesis allows you to focus on a specific aspect of the topic and thereby gives you a good idea of what to look for in each source. When working with a book or even a long magazine article, you can save a lot of time and avoid confusion if you have a definite idea of what is likely to prove useful and what is not.

Whether your hypothesis is right or wrong (or at least not completely accurate) is not your primary concern in the early stages of research. What is important is that you begin as early as possible to think about your topic in increasingly precise terms. This process is the natural result of forming a hypothesis.

Sometimes continued brainstorming and background reading may suggest a topic and a hypothesis at the same time. Here are two examples, showing how writers moved from subjects to topics and possible hypotheses by using brainstorming. In the first example, the student who had brainstormed about dinosaurs was able, after a little background reading, to reject some topics that she had considered earlier. She then narrowed her topic through further brainstorming, and arrived at a hypothesis.

Subject: *the extinction of dinosaurs*

Questions: Did the evolution of small, intelligent animals somehow cause the extinction of dinosaurs? Did major geographical changes lead to the dinosaurs' extinction by eliminating the enormous tropical swamplands in which most of them lived? Did radiation from outer space kill off the dinosaurs? Did dinosaurs become so large that they could not find enough food in their environment?

Topic: *the role of mammals in the extinction of dinosaurs*

Hypothesis: "The dinosaurs became extinct because they could not compete with newly evolved mammals." (The student later changed her hypothesis to "Cosmic radiation killed off the dinosaurs but not all the newly evolved mammals of the time." Her initial hypothesis, however, provided a helpful focus for her reading of sources and led directly to her revised hypothesis.)

Subject: *treatment of alcohol addiction*

Questions: How well do support therapies, such as Alcoholics Anonymous, work in their efforts to cure alcoholism? How successful are aversion therapies that use chemicals to make liquor repellent? How successful are cognitive therapies that attempt to get alcoholics to disapprove of their behavior when drinking? How effective is psychotherapy that deals with the alcoholic's unconscious reasons for drinking?

Topic: *cognitive therapy for alcoholism*

Hypothesis: "If alcoholics can be shown their true behavior when drunk, they can learn to disapprove of drinking and be cured of alcoholism." (The student modified this optimistic view after reading several sources but nonetheless benefited from the focus provided by the initial hypothesis.)

TWO STUDENTS FORM THEIR HYPOTHESES

What about our two students? George Pitman formed his hypothesis in the process of choosing his topic. He had always thought Jefferson Davis something of a hero, but the article on Davis in the *Encyclopedia Americana* was rather negative about Davis's achievements, and so Pitman assumed that the majority of Civil War historians would take this view. He therefore adopted the hypothesis, "Jefferson Davis's weaknesses as a leader contributed significantly to the defeat of the South."

Susanna Andrews thought she had a good topic, but she had found no solid basis in her background reading for forming a hypothesis. She spent a little time brainstorming about her topic:

Why did Dickinson refuse to publish most of her poems? Why would anyone refuse? Did she think they weren't good enough? Was she too shy to let the world see her thoughts? Did she ever *try* to get the poems published? Who did she permit to read them, and what did those people say? Why did she write poetry anyway—what did writing mean to her? What would publication have involved for her and her poems? When and how did the poems actually come to be published?

These questions still did not give the student a hypothesis, but they suggested that the answer might lie in Dickinson's attitude toward poetry and toward herself. The instructor in the course on modern poetry had pointed out that these were themes of some Dickinson poems, so the student reread some of the poetry and was struck by these lines: "The Soul selects her own Society— / Then—shuts the Door—. . ." Since background reading had shown that the poet was extremely shy, Susanna Andrews decided to use as a hypothesis, "Emily Dickinson chose not to publish her poems because she was a shy, reclusive person who was not interested in public acclaim."

As you have seen, neither hypothesis was to become the thesis of a finished paper. In each case, the student's research into specialized sources disclosed new information and more persuasive arguments in support of another thesis. Of what use, then, is a hypothesis? Why guess, when so often your guess will be wrong? There are two good reasons for forming a hypothesis, even if that hypothesis does prove to be wrong. First, your hypothesis may not be the actual statement you finally use as your thesis, but it is the same *kind* of statement, and therefore will help you to decide what kind of information—out of all the information you will uncover—is relevant to your purposes. Second, the hypothesis is a useful tool for testing the thoroughness of your research. If in reading about Jefferson Davis, for example, George Pitman had found nothing but praise for Davis's conduct of the Confederate presidency, obviously something would have been wrong with his research, since general reference books like the *Encyclopedia Americana* do not invent "facts" or include completely unsubstantiated interpretations.

Remember, you have a limited amount of time to spend reading and taking notes. A sufficiently narrow topic will ensure that you will be working with a manageable number of sources, and a hypothesis will help you to decide what material in each source will be most useful to you when you write the paper. A carefully chosen topic and a reasonable hypothesis are essential if you are to control the time and effort you will expend throughout the research process.

Some General Reference Sources

Here are some reference books which you will find in many college libraries and which you can use for background reading in your subject.

GENERAL ENCYCLOPEDIAS

Collier's Encyclopedia. 24 vols. with annual supplements. New York: Macmillan Educational Corp., 1981.

Encyclopedia Americana. 30 vols. with annual supplements. New York: Encyclopedia Americana, 1978. Emphasizes subjects related to the United States.

New Columbia Encyclopedia, The. 4th ed. 1 vol. New York: Columbia University Press, 1975.

New Encyclopaedia Britannica, The. 15th ed. 30 vols. with annual supplements. Chicago: Encyclopaedia Britannica, 1974. Editions prior to the current edition emphasized subjects related to Great Britain and Europe.

ART AND ARCHITECTURE

Encyclopedia of World Art. 15 vols. New York: McGraw-Hill, 1959–68. Guide.

McGraw-Hill Dictionary of Art. Ed. Bernard S. Myers and Shirley D. Myers. 5 vols. New York: McGraw-Hill, 1969.

Praeger Encyclopedia of Art. 5 vols. Chicago: Encyclopaedia Britannica, 1971.

ASTRONOMY

Cambridge Encyclopedia of Astronomy. The Institute of Astronomy, University of Cambridge. New York: Crown, 1977.

Satterthwaite, Gilbert E., ed. *Encyclopedia of Astronomy.* New York: St. Martin's, 1971.

BIOGRAPHY

Chambers's Biographical Dictionary. Ed. J. O. Thorne. Rev. ed. T. C. Collocott. 2 vols. New York: Two Continents, 1974.

Current Biography. New York: H. W. Wilson, 1940–present. Published monthly with annual and ten-year cumulations into volumes.

Dictionary of American Biography. 21 vols. New York: Scribner's, 1928–37. Supplement One (through 1935); Supplement Two (1936–40).

Dictionary of National Biography. Ed. Leslie Stephen and Sidney Lee. 22 vols. London: Oxford University Press, 1922. Including supplements through 1970. Ed. George Smith. Detailed biographies of deceased Britons.

Directory of American Scholars. 7th ed. 3 vols. Ed. Jacques Cattell Press. New York: Bowker, 1978.

Notable American Women 1607–1950: A Biographical Dictionary. Ed. Edward T. James and Janet W. James. 3 vols. Cambridge, Mass.: Belknap Press, Harvard University Press, 1971.

Who's Who. London: A. & C. Black; New York: St. Martin's, 1849–present (annual). Mainly British.

Who's Who in America. Chicago: Marquis-Who's Who, 1899–present (biennial).

Who's Who in the World. 5th ed. Chicago: Marquis-Who's Who, 1980.

BIOLOGY

Gray, Peter, ed. *Encyclopedia of Biological Sciences.* 2nd ed. New York: Van Nostrand Reinhold, 1970.

BUSINESS

Clark, Donald T., and Bert A. Gottfried. *University Dictionary of Business and Finance.* New York: Thomas Y. Crowell, 1957.

CHEMISTRY

Hampel, Clifford A., and Gessner G. Hawley, eds. *Encyclopedia of Chemistry.* 3rd ed. New York: Reinhold, 1973.

DRAMA

Hartnoll, Phyllis, ed. *The Oxford Companion to the Theater.* 3rd ed. New York: Oxford University Press, 1967.

Matlaw, Myron. *Modern World Drama: An Encyclopedia.* New York: Dutton, 1972.

McGraw-Hill Encyclopedia of World Drama. 4 vols. New York: McGraw-Hill, 1972.

ECONOMICS

Cambridge Economic History of Europe, The. 7 vols. New York: Cambridge University Press, 1965.

Greenwald, Douglas, and Associates, *McGraw-Hill Dictionary of Modern Economics: A Handbook of Terms and Organizations.* New York: McGraw-Hill, 1973.

Nemmers, Erwin E., ed. *Dictionary of Economics and Business.* 4th enl. ed. Totowa, N.J.: Littlefield, 1978.

EDUCATION

Encyclopedia of Education. Ed. Lee C. Deighton, et al. 10 vols. New York: Macmillan, 1971.

Good, Carter Victor, ed. *Dictionary of Education.* 3rd ed. New York: McGraw-Hill, 1973.

ENGINEERING

Jones, Franklin D., and Paul B. Schubert. *Engineering Encyclopedia.* 3rd ed. New York: Industrial Press, 1963.

Perry, Robert H., ed. *Engineering Manual: A Practical Reference of Design.* 3rd ed. New York: McGraw-Hill, 1976.

Schenck, Hilbert. *Introduction to the Engineering Research Project.* New York: McGraw-Hill, 1969.

ENVIRONMENTAL SCIENCE

Encyclopedia of Ecology. Ed. Bernhard Grzimek. New York: Van Nostrand Reinhold, 1976.

Lapedes, Daniel N., ed. *Encyclopedia of Environmental Science.* New York: McGraw-Hill, 1974.

HISTORY

Bury, J. B., et al., eds. *Cambridge Ancient History.* 2nd ed. 12 vols. New York: Macmillan, 1923–39. (Third edition in progress.)

Cambridge Medieval History. Ed. H. M. Gwathin, et al. 8 vols. New York: Macmillan, 1911–36. (Second edition in progress.)

Cambridge Modern History. Ed. A. W. Ward, et al. 13 vols. New York: Macmillan, 1902–22.

Langer, William Leonard, ed. *Encyclopedia of World History: Ancient, Medieval, and Modern Chronologically Arranged,* 5th ed. Boston: Houghton Mifflin, 1972.

New Cambridge Modern History. Ed. G. R. Potter. 14 vols. New York: Cambridge University Press, 1970.

See also Political Science.

LANGUAGE (ENGLISH) AND LINGUISTICS

Hayes, Curtis W., Jacob Ornstein, and William W. Gage. *The ABC's of Languages and Linguistics.* Rev. ed. Silver Spring, Md.: Institute of Modern Languages, 1977.

Pyles, Thomas. *The Origins and Development of the English Language.* 2nd ed. New York: Harcourt Brace Jovanovich, 1971.

Slobin, Dan I. *Psycholinguistics,* 2nd ed. Glenview, Ill.: Scott Foresman, 1979.

LITERATURE

Bede, Jean-Albert, and William Edgerton, eds. *Columbia Dictionary of Modern European Literature,* 2nd ed. New York: Columbia University Press, 1980.

Cassell's Encyclopedia of World Literature. Ed. J. Buchanan-Brown. Rev. ed. New York: Morrow, 1973.

Feder, Lillian, ed. *Crowell's Handbook of Classical Literature.* New York: Thomas Y. Crowell, 1964.

Hart, James David. *The Oxford Companion to American Literature*. 4th ed. New York: Oxford University Press, 1965.

Oxford Companion to English Literature, The. Ed. Paul Harvey. Rev. ed. Dorothy Eagle. New York: Oxford University Press, 1967.

Oxford History of English Literature, The. 12 vols. New York: Oxford University Press, 1947–78. Other volumes in preparation.

Spiller, Robert E., et al. *The Literary History of the United States*. 4th ed. 2 vols. New York: Macmillan, 1974.

MEDIA

Educational Media Year Book 1980. 6th ed. Ed. James W. Brown and Shirley N. Brown. New York: 1980. Annual review of developments in educational media.

Rivers, William L., et al. *The Mass Media and Modern Society*. 2nd ed. New York: Holt, Rinehart and Winston, 1971.

MUSIC

New Grove Dictionary of Music and Musicians. 20 vols. Ed. Stanley Sadie. Washington, D.C.: Grove's Dictionaries of Music, 1980.

Scholes, Percy A., ed. *The Oxford Companion to Music*. 10th ed. Rev. ed. John Owen Ward. New York: Oxford University Press, 1970.

Westrup, J. A., and F. L. Harrison, *New College Encyclopedia of Music*. Rev. ed. Conrad Wilson. New York: Norton, 1976.

PHILOSOPHY

Copleston, Frederick. *A History of Philosophy*. 9 vols. New York: Paulist Press, 1976.

Edwards, Paul, ed. *Encyclopedia of Philosophy*. 4 vols. New York: Macmillan, 1973.

PHYSICS

Besancon, Robert M., ed. *Encyclopedia of Physics*. 2nd ed. New York: Van Nostrand Reinhold, 1974.

Fluegge, E., ed. *Encyclopedia of Physics*. 54 vols. New York: Springer-Verlag, 1957–present.

POLITICAL SCIENCE

Plano, Jack C., and Milton Greenberg. *American Political Dictionary*. 5th ed. New York: Holt, Rinehart and Winston, 1979.

Worldmark Encyclopedia of the Nations. 5th ed. 5 vols. New York: Worldmark Press and Harper & Row, 1976.

Yearbook of World Affairs. Published under auspices of London Institute of World Affairs. Boulder, Colo.: Praeger/Westview, 1947–present (annual).

PSYCHOLOGY

Beigel, Hugo G. *Dictionary of Psychology and Related Fields.* New York: Ungar, 1974.
Eysenck, H. J., ed. *Encyclopedia of Psychology,* 2nd ed. 3 vols. New York: Continuum, 1979.
Goldenson, Robert M., ed. *The Encyclopedia of Human Behavior: Psychology, Psychiatry, and Mental Health.* 2 vols. New York: Doubleday, 1970.

RELIGION

Hastings, James, ed. *Encyclopedia of Religion and Ethics.* 12 vols. New York: Scribner's, 1961.
Zaehner, Robert C., ed. *Concise Encyclopedia of Living Faiths.* New York: Hawthorn, 1959.

SOCIOLOGY

Encyclopedia of Social Work. Ed. John Turner. New York: National Association of Social Workers, 1977.
Encyclopedia of Sociology. Ed. Gayle Johnson. Guilford, Conn.: Dushkin Press, 1974.

Review Questions

1. Explain the difference between a subject and a topic for a research paper.
2. How suitable as a research topic would each of the following items be? Explain why each item would be a good or poor selection.
   - the effect of the weather front on observation of the solar eclipse at Brandon, Manitoba, in 1979
   - how FM radio signals are sent and received
   - the FBI in peace and war
   - women in business
   - how bees make honey
   - the colonization of Africa during the nineteenth century
   - laetrile: quackery or a reasonable alternative for those terminally ill with cancer?

3. What is the purpose of brainstorming, not only before but during and after your preliminary research?

4. What is the purpose of background reading?

5. Why should you look for controversial issues when you are trying to find a topic?

6. Explain how the function of a hypothesis differs from that of a thesis.

Exercises

1. Read this article on "Mother" Jones, which appeared in *Notable American Women*, an excellent background resource for topics in women's studies. Find several topics, suitable for a seven- to ten-page research paper, and for each topic, think of a potential hypothesis.

> **JONES, Mary Harris** (May 1, 1830–Nov. 30, 1930), labor agitator, known as "Mother" Jones, was born in Cork, Ireland, to Richard and Helen Harris. Her father emigrated to the United States in 1835 and, on acquiring citizenship, arranged for his wife and children to follow him. Mary Harris attended common school and normal school in Toronto, Canada, where her father took the family while he worked as a railroad construction laborer. She first taught in a convent in Monroe, Mich., but soon went to Chicago to operate a dressmaking business. She was drawn back into teaching in Memphis, Tenn., and there in 1861 was married to "a staunch member" of the Iron Molders' Union named Jones. Her husband and their four small children died in an epidemic of yellow fever that ravaged Memphis in 1867. After serving as a volunteer nurse until the disease was halted, the bereft widow returned to Chicago and resumed dressmaking. As she worked on the clothes of families of wealth, she began to resent economic and social inequities. Burned out of all her possessions by the Chicago Fire of 1871, she found a measure of comfort at the scorched hall of the Knights of Labor, whose meetings she attended. She saw the early labor leaders as "saints and martyrs," and thereafter she committed herself increasingly to their struggle against low wages, long hours, and depressed working conditions. In 1877 she went to Pittsburgh to help striking railroad employees and was there at the time of the bitter riots in which large amounts of railroad property were burned by a mob—damage for which the strikers were blamed. "Labor," she wrote afterward, "must bear the cross for others' sins" (*Autobiography*, p. 16).

From 1880 her course was set. Without a fixed home, finding her lodging where she went, she moved from one industrial area to another, whichever seemed hardest hit by economic depression or labor strife. Where there was a strike, she organized and aided the workers; where there was none, she held educational meetings. Beginning in the early 1890's, her thin, wiry figure became especially identified with the struggles of the coal miners. As an organizer for the United Mine Workers she participated in the anthracite strikes of 1900 and 1902 and attracted widespread public attention to the strikers' wives by leading them in marches on which they routed strikebreakers with brooms and mops. She disapproved of the general settlement that followed President Theodore Roosevelt's intervention, feeling that union recognition could have been achieved.

The production of bituminous coal in West Virginia was omitted from the agreements which the United Mine Workers made with operators in the other Eastern fields. Mother Jones took the lead in organizing unions in that state, first in the northern (Fairmont) district and later in the New River coal camps. In 1903 she broke off an organizing journey through West Virginia to go to Colorado, where, disguised as a peddler, she collected information that led to a walkout in that exploited area. When the Mine Workers' president, John Mitchell, disavowed the strike, she publicly condemned him and quit her union job. Now she made a round of trouble spots farther west. She joined with striking machinists of the Southern Pacific Railroad and gave firsthand support to the Western Federation of Miners when it closed the copper pits in Arizona. While in the Southwest, she became concerned with the plight of Mexican revolutionists then imprisoned in this country, personally carried their case to the White House, and helped secure a Congressional inquiry into their fate. In other instances, too, she demonstrated a special ability to win publicity and governmental attention for the cause of the workers. A notable instance came in 1903 when, to dramatize the evils of child labor, she conducted a caravan of striking children on an overland march from the textile mills of Kensington, Pa., to the home of President Theodore Roosevelt at Oyster Bay, N.Y. At times during the following two years she secured employment in cotton mills in Alabama, Georgia, and South Carolina, in order to gain personal knowledge of child labor conditions in those states.

Renewed appeals to help the coal miners proved irresistible, and in 1911 she was back in West Virginia organizing local unions. Following the mine strike of 1912–13 she was tried by a state militia military court, convicted on a charge of conspiracy to commit murder, and sentenced to prison for twenty years. Labor circles protested strongly, and a Senate investigation was voted, but before it began Mother Jones was freed by the newly elected governor of West Virginia. When new troubles broke out in the Colorado coal mines late in 1913 she went west again. Three times coal operators locked her up and deported her from their properties, and each time she returned to the scene of risk and danger. The machine-gun "massacre" of mine families in a tent colony at Ludlow, Colo., on Apr. 20, 1914, when twenty lives were lost, stirred her as had no other single burst of violence. She told the tragic story to audiences across the country, to members of the House Mines and Mining Committee in Washington, and to President Wilson, who responded by proposing to the union and the owners that they agree to a truce and the creation of a grievance committee at each mine.

Mother Jones reached the age of eighty-five in the period of World War I, but there was little diminution in her efforts. She was in the thick of New York City's streetcar and garment strikes of 1915–16 and the 1919 steel strike. In 1921 she attended the Pan American Federation of Labor meeting in Mexico, her third visit to that country as a representative at an international labor gathering. Even at ninety-one she could be found in the unpainted dwellings of the company towns in West Virginia, encouraging a new generation of mine men and women to play a part in the class struggle as she saw it.

The hundredth anniversary of her birth, May 1, 1930, was celebrated with a reception at the Silver Spring, Md., home of her friend Mrs. Walter Burgess, with whom she lived out her last years. Messages poured in from around the country. White-haired, her small frame dressed in the long-familiar black, she spoke with her old vigor into a talking-picture camera. Thanking John D. Rockefeller, Jr., for a message of congratulations, she recalled her battles at the Rockefeller-owned mines of Colorado and said: "He's a damn good sport. I've licked him many times, but we've made peace." As she had fallen out with John Mitchell, so she parted company with John L. Lewis; after her hundredth birthday she sent $1,000 of the money she had accumulated from gifts and organizing work to aid an insurgent group of Illinois miners who were seeking to oust Lewis from the presidency of the United Mine Workers. She died at Silver Spring seven months after her centennial birthday. After a high requiem mass in Washington, D.C., her body was taken to the bituminous coal fields of southern Illinois, where, at Mount Olive, in the Union Miners Cemetery, she was buried near the graves of victims of the Virden, Ill., mine riot of 1898.

Always an individualist, Mother Jones was a born crusader, with a crusader's inability to compromise, even with her allies. An activist, she lacked a consistent philosophy, but her simple view of the class struggle took her normally into the socialist camp. Though, as she wrote, she "never endorsed" the doctrines of anarchism as she had heard them preached in Chicago at the time of the Haymarket affair, and though she refused in the 1890's to join the Ruskin cooperative colony in Tennessee, she helped found the Social Democratic party in 1898 and was one of the organizers of the Industrial Workers of the World in 1905. Yet, in cooperation with the American Federation of Labor, she campaigned in the coalmine areas of Indiana in 1916 for the Democratic ticket. She made her last major public address at the 1924 convention of the Farmer-Labor party. She opposed woman suffrage. "The plutocrats," she wrote, "have organized their women. They keep them busy with suffrage and prohibition and charity" (*Autobiography,* p. 204).

The labor writer Tom Tippett, who saw Mother Jones at first hand, wrote that she was out of place in the union office because of her quarrelsome habits and lack of constructive policy. Noting that she made her real contribution in the field, he said: "With one speech she often threw a whole community on strike and she could keep the strikers loyal month after month on empty stomachs and behind prison bars" (*Encyclopedia of the Social Sciences,* VIII, 415). Above all she was passionately humane, and this quality, as much as her utter fearlessness, brought her success where others had failed.

[The *Autobiog. of Mother Jones* (1925), edited by Mary F. Parton, is the fullest account of her life, but there are inaccuracies. See also Elsie Glück, *John Mitchell, Miner* (1929); McAlister Coleman, *Men and Coal* (1943); Paul F. Brissenden, *The I.W.W.* (1919); Ralph Chaplin, *Wobbly* (1948); *Proc.* of conventions of United Mine Workers; testimony before U.S. Commission on Industrial Relations, *Senate Doc. No. 415,* 64 Cong., 1 Sess., vol. XI (1915–16); Ray Ginger, *The Bending Cross* (1949); Howard H. Quint, *The Forging of Am. Socialism* (1953); Robert J. Cornell, *The Anthracite Coal Strike of 1902* (1957); Edward M. Steel, "Mother Jones in the Fairmont Field, 1902," *Jour. of Am. Hist.,* Sept. 1970. The periodical and newspaper literature is voluminous, for example: *Current Opinion,* July 1913; *Outlook,* Feb. 3, 10, 1915; *New Republic,* Feb. 20, 1915; *Nation,* July 19, 1922; *N.Y. Times,* June 1, 1913, May 2, 1930, Dec. 1, 2, 1930; *United Mine Workers Jour.,* Dec. 15, 1930; *Labor* (Washington), Dec. 9, 1930; *Labor Clarion* (San Francisco), Dec. 5, 1930; *Labor's News,* Dec. 13, 1930; *Labor Age,* Jan. 1931. Information on certain points from Prof. Edward M. Steel, W. Va. Univ.]

IRVING DILLIARD
MARY SUE DILLIARD SCHUSKY

2. From each of the two lists that follow, choose a subject that interests you. Using references in your library, find three suitable topics for each subject and a hypothesis for each topic. In addition
to articles in general encyclopedias, consult reference books covering specific fields. If you have difficulty finding the sources that
you need, ask a librarian for assistance.

List A

animistic religions
Asian immigrants into the
   United States
the banking industry and the
   Great Depression
economic inflation
endangered species
environmental controls and
   chemical industries
European colonization of
   Africa
extrasensory perception (ESP)
fundamentalist religions
genetic engineering

group therapy for emotional
   problems
impressionist artists
the Iranian revolution of 1979
nineteenth-century Italian
   opera
organized crime
prehistoric American peoples
school desegregation
twentieth-century music
the United States judicial
   system
urban problems

List B

Aristotle, philosopher
Samuel Beckett, playwright
Maria Callas, soprano
Cesar Chavez, union leader
Marie Curie, scientist
Charles Darwin, naturalist
John Foster Dulles, American
   diplomat and statesman
Marcus Garvey, black
   nationalist
Robert Hutchings Goddard,
   physicist and rocket expert
Carl Jung, psychologist

John Maynard Keynes,
   economist
Le Corbusier, architect
Malcolm X, black militant
Golda Meir, Israeli political
   leader
Eleanor Roosevelt,
   humanitarian
Igor Stravinsky, composer
Walt Whitman, poet
Virginia Woolf, writer
Richard Wright, writer
Andrew Wyeth, painter

3

Using the Library

After you have chosen a research topic and formed a hypothesis about it, you are ready to take the next step: making a list of sources dealing with your topic. You may already have begun your list by noting items found in the bibliographies in the general references you read when choosing your topic, but those bibliographies are usually very limited and sometimes out of date, and your library may not have copies of all the sources. What you need now is a list of sources that your library actually has on its shelves for you to use in your research.

To compile that list, you will need to become familiar with the way sources are catalogued in your library. All library catalogs follow a standard organizational plan; if you know how to use one of them, you can find your way in any other. And most libraries have the same basic indexes to articles in magazines and newspapers. This chapter provides an overview of the library catalog and the main periodical indexes. The next chapter will show how to use these resources when working on your research paper.

Working with Librarians

It is a good idea to introduce yourself early to the reference librarian and to describe your project briefly. The reference librarian can tell you about any special resources available in the library and can often help you to solve problems quickly that might take hours to solve on your own. Librarians are professionals trained not only in managing libraries but in finding sources on many subjects, and it is their job to help people with research projects. The research librarian might even have helped someone else working on a topic related to yours and be able to give you hints and suggestions that will lead you to valuable sources you might otherwise miss.

Nevertheless, you must remember that although most librarians are quite willing to assist you with your research, they are not obliged to do your research paper for you. You should not go to the librarian and say, "I have to do a paper for my American history course, but I don't know what to write about. Can you help me to get some books?" The librarian has not attended your classes or read your textbooks and cannot invent a topic for you. If you are at a loss for a topic, see your instructor, not your librarian.

Kinds of Sources

In your research you will be working mainly with books and periodicals. (A periodical is a publication that appears regularly under the same title: *Washington Post, Newsweek, Science News, PMLA (Publications of the Modern Language Association),* and so on.) Books are catalogued and shelved in one way, periodicals in another, and most of this chapter is about how to find sources of each kind.

Many students think of library research as pertaining only to books, but periodical articles offer several important advantages. A book takes many months or even years to write, and months more to be published, so that it may be at least partly out of date by the time it first appears, and still more so by the time you read it. Articles can be published much more quickly, and in some fields where information and interpretations change rapidly, such as science and technology, articles have replaced books as the main way that professionals exchange information and ideas. Even in fields such as history and literature, you need to check the periodical indexes to make sure your research is up to date. And subjects in current affairs, such as *government energy policy* and *the Equal Rights Amendment,* will have to be researched mainly in such periodicals as newspapers, news magazines, and journals of political commentary.

Another advantage of periodical articles is that they usually deal with specific topics in a narrower but deeper way than might a book. For example, a book about the world's food supply might include a chapter on innovative proposals for increasing agricultural production, but only a paragraph or two might be about "farming" the ocean floor. But in your library there are probably many recent articles on ocean farming which cover the topic in much greater detail and depth. Furthermore, since a periodical article usually focuses on a specific topic, its title can often tell you exactly what that topic is, and save you time in your search for relevant sources. If you were planning a paper on ocean farming, titles like these would immediately catch your eye:

"A Proposal for Implementing Ocean Farming Off the Southeastern Coast of the United States"

"Ocean Farming: The Crop Will Not Cover the Cost"

Besides books and periodicals, your library may have other kinds of sources on your topic. Some are published or reproduced in microform, such as microfilm and microfiche, and reading them requires special machines. Others may be unpublished materials such as manuscripts, letters, and diaries. Still others may not be written at all—sound recordings and pictorial material, for example. The librarian will know the special sources that are in the library and whether these sources will help you in your research.

As long as you are working with books and periodicals, however, you can compile most of your list of sources without the librarian's help. Books are listed in the library's card catalog, which we will describe first. Magazine articles are not entered in the card catalog but are found through various published indexes; these we will describe next. At the end of the chapter we will describe other kinds of sources and how to find them.

The Library Card Catalog

You probably already know that the library card catalog is an alphabetical index, made up of three-by-five-inch file cards, that lists information about all the books in the library. Actually, there are more cards in the card catalog than the library has books, because at least two and often three or more cards are filed for each book:

1. an *author* card
2. a *title* card
3. one or more *subject* cards (optional)

In some libraries the author and title cards are in one set of cabinet drawers and the subject cards in another. In other libraries all the cards are interfiled.

Many books are listed under more than one subject heading. For example, in one library, Bruce Catton's *Grant Takes Command* can be found under these headings:

1. (author)   CATTON, Bruce

2. (title)   *Grant Takes Command*

3. (subject)   Grant, Ulysses S. (1822–85)

4. (subject)   Civil War—Military Leaders

The card catalog may also include cross-reference cards that list subject headings under which related materials can be found. A cross-reference or "see also" card, such as that in Figure 3–1, is filed at the end of a set of subject cards.

were you interested only in the Civil War, you would not consult "Reconstruction period" or "PRESIDENTS"

```
GRANT, Ulysses S.   (1822-85)

      see also

U.S.--HISTORY--CIVIL WAR
   Military leaders
   Reconstruction period
U.S.--PRESIDENTS
```

Figure 3–1. A "see also" card

A cross-reference card can help you find sources that you might otherwise miss. For example, if you were planning a paper on the topic *Grant's new style of warfare,* a book titled *Lincoln Finds a General* could be quite useful, for the book deals with Lincoln's search for a commander who would wage the war in a particular way—and of course Grant was his choice. This book, however, might well be catalogued only under "CIVIL WAR—Military Leaders" and not under "GRANT." Without the cross-reference card, you might overlook a valuable source.

FINDING A CARD

In compiling a list of sources, you will often begin looking for subject cards whose subjects are related to your topic. For example, if you were looking for sources about the Civil War, you might first look under

"Civil War." There you would probably find a cross-reference card telling you to look under "U.S.—HISTORY—CIVIL WAR." Looking there, you would find a number of cards like that in Figure 3–2.

subject heading is typed at the top of the card

E
468
R27
	U.S.--HISTORY--CIVIL WAR
	Randall, James Garfield, 1881-1953.
	    The divided Union ₍by₎ J. G. Randall ₍and₎ David Donald
	Boston, Little, Brown ₍1961₎
	
	    xvi, 572 p. illus., ports, maps. 24 cm
	    Based on "the late J. G. Randall's The Civil War and Reconstruction."
	    Bibliography: p. ₍533₎-548.
	
	    1. U.S.–Hist.–Civil War. I. Randall, James Garfield, 1881-1953.
	The Civil War and Reconstruction. II. Donald, David Herbert, 1920–
	III. Title.
	
	    E468.R27 973.7 61-9295

Figure 3–2. A subject card

If your topic is more specific, such as Jefferson Davis, you would probably do better to look for a subject card on Davis himself: "Davis, Jefferson, 1808–1889."

To locate an author card, look in the catalog under the author's last name; then, if necessary, use his or her other names. The author card for *The Divided Union* is shown in Figure 3–3.

except for the subject heading, card is identical to subject card and is listed under author's name

E
468
R27
	Randall, James Garfield, 1881-1953.
	    The divided Union ₍by₎ J. G. Randall ₍and₎ David Donald
	Boston, Little, Brown ₍1961₎
	
	    xvi, 572 p. illus., ports, maps. 24 cm
	    Based on "the late J. G. Randall's The Civil War and Reconstruction."
	    Bibliography: p. ₍533₎-548.
	
	    1. U.S.–Hist.–Civil War. I. Randall, James Garfield, 1881-1953.
	The Civil War and Reconstruction. II. Donald, David Herbert, 1920–
	III. Title.
	
	    E468.R27 973.7 61-9295

Figure 3–3. An author card

This card looks the same as the subject card, except that it lacks the subject heading typed across the top. It is filed under *Randall*.

To locate a title card, look for the first word in the title of the book, omitting *A, An,* or *The.* The title card for Randall's book on the Civil War looks like this:

The title card looks the same as the author card except that the title is typed across the top. It is filed under *Divided Union*—not under *The.* See Figure 3–4.

card is identical to
subject and author
cards except for
title typed at its top

```
E          The divided Union.
468      Randall, James Garfield, 1881–1953.
R27          The divided Union ₍by₎ J. G. Randall ₍and₎ David Donald
             Boston, Little, Brown ₍1961₎

             xvi, 572 p. illus., ports, maps. 24 cm

             Based on "the late J. G. Randall's The Civil War and Reconstruction."
             Bibliography: p. ₍533₎–548.


             1.  U.S.–Hist.–Civil War.  I.  Randall, James Garfield, 1881–1953.
             The Civil War and Reconstruction.  II.  Donald, David Herbert, 1920–
             III.  Title.

             E468.R27                      973.7                    61-9295
```

Figure 3–4. A title card

It will help you to know two other alphabetical rules:

1. Abbreviations are alphabetized as if they were spelled out. For example, *St.* is filed under *Saint.*

2. *Mc,* as in *McAllister,* is alphabetized as if it were spelled *Mac.*

UNDERSTANDING A CATALOG CARD

Because the information on a catalog card is presented in a standardized way, you will have to understand the format, and the significance of the various pieces of information, if the card is to help you. On the following author card, ten key pieces of information are identified in Figure 3–5.

Three items—call number, author's name, and book title—are essential to your search for sources. The remaining seven items may also be useful to you when you evaluate sources for possible use in your research paper.

Locating Books

Once you have decided which books you should read, locating the actual books within the library is usually not very difficult. In most libraries, the books are shelved according to call numbers based on one

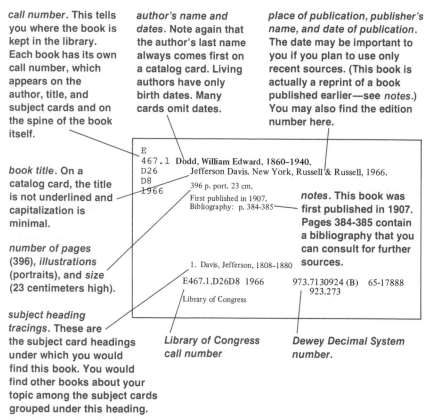

call number. This tells you where the book is kept in the library. Each book has its own call number, which appears on the author, title, and subject cards and on the spine of the book itself.

author's name and dates. Note again that the author's last name always comes first on a catalog card. Living authors have only birth dates. Many cards omit dates.

place of publication, publisher's name, and date of publication. The date may be important to you if you plan to use only recent sources. (This book is actually a reprint of a book published earlier—see notes.) You may also find the edition number here.

book title. On a catalog card, the title is not underlined and capitalization is minimal.

number of pages (396), illustrations (portraits), and size (23 centimeters high).

subject heading tracings. These are the subject card headings under which you would find this book. You would find other books about your topic among the subject cards grouped under this heading.

notes. This book was first published in 1907. Pages 384-385 contain a bibliography that you can consult for further sources.

Library of Congress call number

Dewey Decimal System number.

E
467.1 Dodd, William Edward, 1860–1940.
D26   Jefferson Davis. New York, Russell & Russell, 1966.
D8
1966   396 p. port. 23 cm.
            First published in 1907.
            Bibliography: p. 384-385

            1. Davis, Jefferson, 1808–1880

            E467.1.D26D8 1966   973.7130924 (B)   65-17888
                                                  923.273
            Library of Congress

Figure 3–5. An annotated author card

of two major classification systems: the *Library of Congress* or the *Dewey Decimal.*

The Library of Congress system uses a combination of letters and numbers to arrange books by subject area. The Dewey Decimal system uses numbers to designate major subject areas, and then a combination of letters and numbers to designate subdivisions under the major classifications. You do not have to memorize the codes for the system your library uses, and you need no specialized knowledge to use it yourself. If you have access to the stacks where the books are kept, familiarizing yourself with the call numbers for your particular field will enable you both to locate the books you have found in the card catalog and to browse in appropriate sections for other books that may prove valuable. As always, your librarian is trained to help you if you have any problems understanding the organization and location of materials in the library.

CLOSED STACKS

Some libraries allow you access to the book shelves; others do not. In order to get books in libraries whose stacks are closed to you, you must fill out a *call slip* and present it to a library employee who will find the book and give it to you. A call slip usually asks for basic information which you must copy from the catalog card for the book.

BOOKS ON RESERVE

Most college libraries have a *reserve reading room*. This room contains books that instructors have asked a librarian to set aside for their classes. A book placed on reserve cannot be checked out of the library or, at best, can only be taken out overnight. When a book is put on reserve, a librarian usually notes that on the catalog cards that list the book. If you discover that a book you need for your research has been put on reserve, you should plan to read it and take notes on it in the library. Try to use reserve books as early in the term as possible, for you can be sure that other students will soon be competing with you to consult the same books.

Periodical Indexes

Specific articles published in magazines and newspapers are not listed in the library's card catalog but in guides known as periodical indexes. Recent articles are catalogued at intervals throughout the year in paperbound supplements to the past year's index. At the end of the year complete annual indexes appear as one or two hardbound volumes. These volumes, as well as the periodical supplements, are usually kept on shelves or tables in the reference room of the library and must be used there.

In a periodical index you will find subject entries and, sometimes, author entries, condensed into abbreviations to save space. Different indexes use different formats and abbreviations and include somewhat different amounts and kinds of information. The meaning of each abbreviation is explained at the beginning of each volume, and you should consult these explanations before using the index.

Once you have found an index entry for an article that promises to be a good source for your paper, you need to find out whether your library has a copy of the periodical in which that article appeared. In some libraries, periodicals are listed alphabetically by title in the card catalog or in a separate periodicals card catalog. In others, periodicals are listed in pamphlets, on loose pages at the main desk, or in computer printouts. Whatever system your library uses, find out from the librarian how it operates.

The library's periodical list may not always tell you whether the library has the particular issue you need. Normally, the list only says how long the library has been accumulating issues of each magazine. The list will also give the location of the periodical and may indicate that some or all issues are available only on microfilm or microfiche.

Types of Periodicals

Periodicals fall into two broad categories—popular and professional—according to their intended audiences. Within each category, you may have to use several indexes, most of which can be found in the reference room of your library.

Some of the most frequently used indexes are

popular periodicals (magazines and newspapers)	*Readers' Guide to Periodical Literature* *New York Times Index* *Book Review Digest*
professional periodicals (often called journals)	*Humanities Index* *Social Sciences Index*

In addition, there are many indexes for periodicals in specific fields, such as art, medicine, and psychology.

Indexes to Popular Periodicals

THE READERS' GUIDE TO PERIODICAL LITERATURE

The *Readers' Guide* is an index to articles on a wide variety of subjects published in periodicals intended primarily for the general reading public. Some periodicals, such as *Newsweek, Reader's Digest,* and *National Geographic,* are aimed at a cross section of American readers. Others, such as *Aviation Week, Business Week,* and *Art in America,* are designed to appeal to special interests. Here are other samples of the 175 magazines indexed by *Readers' Guide* and the subjects they cover:

The American City—architecture, city planning, urban problems

Atlantic Monthly—current affairs, short fiction

Consumer Reports—evaluations of the performances of commercial products for the general reader

Cosmopolitan—primarily for career women

Ebony—items, with illustrations, of particular interest to black readers

Foreign Affairs—political topics, aimed at fairly sophisticated readers

House and Garden—architecture, interior decoration, landscaping

National Review—political issues, aimed at conservative readers

New Republic—political issues, aimed at liberal or moderate readers

Psychology Today—reports on recent research in all branches of psychology, designed for the general reader

Scientific American—reports on recent scientific research, aimed at fairly sophisticated readers

Sports Illustrated—sports and excellent photographs for the general public

Time—news items from the current week for the general public

United Nations Monthly Chronicle—issues pertaining to the work of the United Nations

Vital Speeches of the Day—for those who want to know *exactly* what was said

The *Readers' Guide* is published as a series of volumes, each volume covering one or more years (the *Guide* year now runs from March through February), beginning with 1900. (If you need material from the nineteenth century, go to *Poole's Index to Periodical Literature*, which covers the period from 1802 to 1906.) The *Readers' Guide* is most useful for social science subjects—modern history, economics, political science, and sociology. It is especially valuable for topics that concern public reaction to a past event at the time it was happening, such as Franklin Roosevelt's attempt to alter the composition of the Supreme Court, and for current events that are not yet included in books, such as changing attitudes toward old age in the United States from 1970 to the present.

For scientific topics, the *Readers' Guide* offers relatively few useful sources. Scientific subjects were not even included in this index until 1953. More importantly, because magazines for the general public avoid highly technical discussions, their writers on science often oversimplify and occasionally distort some of the ideas they try to explain. Although you may begin your investigation of a scientific topic with a popular magazine, you should then turn to books and scholarly journals that deal with the same topic.

How to Use the Readers' Guide. The *Readers' Guide* lists both authors and subjects alphabetically. This means that, regardless of whether you are looking for a subject or an author, you use this index as you would a dictionary. For example, if you were looking for periodical articles published during 1977 on the siege of Vicksburg, you would probably first look in the 1977–1978 *Guide* under "Civil War" and find the cross-reference shown in Figure 3–6.

Under the heading "United States—History," you would find the

CIVIL service pensions
  Burden of generosity. L. Aspin; discussion.
    Harpers 254:4 + F '77
  Rising cost of public pensions—can taxpayers
    afford them? il U.S. News 82:84-6 Ja 24 '77
  Washington memo; key Republicans urge merger
    with Civil Service Retirement Fund to save
    social security. R. D. Westgate, Ret Liv 17:
    60-2 N '77
      See also
  Municipal employees—Pensions

Finance
  See Pensions—Finance
CIVIL war
  See also

The *Guide* directs you
to another heading to
find articles on the
Civil War. The *Guide*
uses the same subject
headings as the library
card catalog.

  Lebanon—Civil War, 1975-
  Spain—History—Civil War, 1936-1939
CIVIL War (United States) See United States—
  History—Civil War, 1861-1865
CIVILIZATION
  Terror of the wilderness; spread of Western
    civilization; excerpt from The cost of living.
    F. Turner. il Am Heritage 28:58-65 F '77
  Toward a day of reckoning: the poor vs. the
    rich worlds. H. Brown. Current 191:23-9 Mr '77
  Tutankhamun and Star trek; address, July 29.
    1977. C. L. Babcock. Vital Speeches 43:744-7
    0 1 '77
  Visions of futures past; Lindisfarne Association.
    S. Helgesen. il Harpers 254:80-6 Mr '77
      See also
  Acculturation
  Animals and civilization
  History
  Popular culture
  Renaissance
  Social change
  Social sciences
  Technology and civilization
      also subhead Civilization under names of
      countries, e.g. France—Civilization

Figure 3–6. From the *Readers' Guide*

subheading "Civil War, 1861–1865—Campaigns and battles," followed by the information you were looking for (Figure 3–7).

To look up an author in the *Readers' Guide,* look alphabetically for the author's last name. All the articles by a particular author are then arranged alphabetically according to the first word of each title, disregarding *A, An,* and *The.* The word *about* above an author's name indicates that the author is the subject of an article written by someone else.

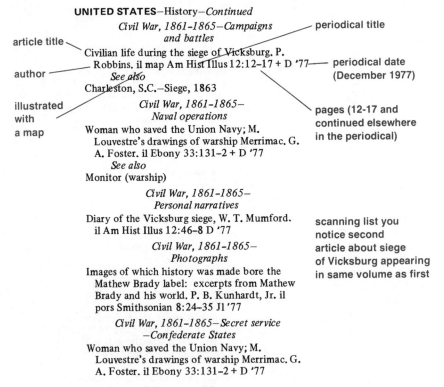

Figure 3–7. From the *Readers' Guide*

THE NEW YORK TIMES INDEX

The *New York Times* is generally agreed to be the most important newspaper in the United States. All major news accounts and feature articles that have appeared in the *Times* since 1913 are indexed in annual volumes of the *New York Times Index,* arranged alphabetically according to subject. To locate articles on a specific topic or event, select the volumes that cover the relevant time period and then look alphabetically in the volumes for the appropriate subject. To check the *Index* for very recent events, use the supplements that are published every two weeks. At the year's end these supplements become part of a new annual volume of the *Index*.

Every daily issue of the *New York Times*, beginning with the very first in 1851, has been preserved on microfilm, and many libraries have a complete set. When you find the date of a particular news item in the *Index*, you can obtain a filmstrip of the *Times* for that date and run it through a microfilm viewer. Even if your library does not subscribe to the *Times* on microfilm, you can consult the *New York Times Index* to find the dates on which important events were reported. You can then use those dates to locate information in those newspapers that your library does have, since most newspapers usually publish important stories at the same time.

The *New York Times Index* offers another convenient feature: it briefly summarizes many articles which may help you decide whether you will find it worthwhile to spend time searching for and reading a particular story.

Figure 3–8 shows a sample from the *New York Times Index*. The entry, "DAVIS, Jefferson" in the annual bound volume of the *New York Times Index* for 1977 indicates that two articles about Jefferson Davis appeared in the newspaper in 1977. Notice that the birth date given for Davis here (1809) differs from that correctly given on page 10 in the encyclopedia article (1808): if this sort of information is important to your research, be sure to check it against the most reliable sources available.

The *New York Times Index* is most useful for social science subjects, such as modern history, economics, and political science. The *Times* also reports extensively on literature and the arts. Newspaper articles are particularly useful for topics that require you to know precisely what facts and impressions were reported at the time an event occurred or to sample public opinion over a particular period of time. Here are some examples of such topics.

> attitudes toward Prohibition at the time the Eighteenth Amendment was being ratified (1917–1919)

> reactions throughout the South to the Supreme Court decision of 1954 outlawing segregation in public schools

> the extent to which the American public was misinformed about the testing of atomic bombs in Nevada after World War II

an article dealing with restoration of Davis's citizenship appeared in section IV, page 9, column 4 of the April 24 issue of the *Times*; "(S)" indicates article was short; medium-length articles are identified "(M)," long articles by "(L)"

an article about the FBI's recovery of objects that once belonged to Davis appeared in May ("My"), on the fifteenth ("15"), on page 51 ("51"), in the third column (":3"); "(S)" indicates article was short

DAVIS, I G. See also Gambling–NJ, Mr 3, My 5, Je 3
DAVIS, Issa, See also Fires–NYC, Jl 16
DAVIS, J B, See also Culture–US, N 3
DAVIS, James (Suspect), See also Murders–NYC, Aguilles, Christian (Ptl), Mr 21
DAVIS, Jefferson (1809–89)
  Sen Judiciary Com approves bill restoring Jefferson Davis's citizenship (S), Ap 24, IV, 9:4; FBI recovers Jefferson Davis's pipe and case, which was stolen from display at Casement Museum, Ft Monroe, Va, 6 days ago and found in Augusta, Ga, in hands of private individual; no arrests reptd (S), My 15,51:3
DAVIS, John H. See also Straus, Roger W Jr, N 27
DAVIS, John M (Judge). See also King, M L, Jl 16
DAVIS, John W 3d (Judge). See also Wallace, George Corley (Gov). S 24, Wallace, George Corley (Mrs). N. J. Wallace, George Corley (Gov). D 6
DAVIS, Joseph (Prisoner). See also Capital Punishment, S 8 Murders–California, N 19 Murders–NYS, Woods, Harold (Ptl), S 8, N 16 D 10.20
DAVIS, Karen (Dr). See also Brookings Institution, Ap 3. Med–US, Ja 6, N 8, Med–US–Health Insurance, Ja 2
DAVIS, Leon. See also Housing–NYC–Cooperatives, F 28
DAVIS, Lewis Carlton. See also Ballet Theater Foundation, Je 13
DAVIS, Lynn. See also US–Defense Dept. Ja 22
DAVIS, Margy-Ruth, See also USSR–Pol. Ap 20
DAVIS, Mark. See also Murders–NYC, Robinson, Steven, Jl 13
DAVIS, Martha. See also Drug addiction–NYC–Therapy, O 24,25
DAVIS, Martin S. See also Athena Communications Corp. Jl 25, Gulf & Western Industries Inc. Jl 26
DAVIS, Martin S. See also Baseball–AL, Oakland Athletics, D 15,16.24,29,31
DAVIS, Mendel J (Repr). See also Louisiana–Elections, O 5
DAVIS, Michael (Ford Motor Co). See also Transit Systems–US, Ag 28
DAVIS, Michael (Shipping Exec). See also Antiques, O 20

Figure 3–8. From the *New York Times Index*

While researching public opinion preceding an event, such as an election or the ratification of a Constitutional amendment, be sure to check the *Index* volume that covers not only the calendar year of the event but the previous year, especially if the event took place early in its year. Similarly, when investigating the reactions to an event, check the *Index* volume for the year of the event and the following year.

THE NEWSPAPER INDEX

A recent addition to periodical guides is the *Newspaper Index,* which began publication in 1972. This index provides information on articles that have appeared in four of the nation's largest newspapers: the *Chicago Tribune,* the *Los Angeles Times,* the *New Orleans Times-Picayune,* and the *Washington Post.* As you might gather from the titles of the newspapers included, this index can be especially useful for looking up regional news and opinion, as well as national and international news.

THE BOOK REVIEW DIGEST

The *Book Review Digest* consists of brief excerpts from book reviews that appeared within a year after a book was first published. The *Book Review Digest* does not cite every published review, but only a sample of critical responses, both favorable and unfavorable.

Each annual volume of this digest (beginning in 1905) indexes reviews of several thousand books, according to both title and author. To use the *Book Review Digest,* you need to know the year in which a book was first published. Then you should look up the title (or the author) in the volumes both for that year and the next year because some books are not reviewed during the calendar year in which they are published: a book published in November 1966, for example, might not have been reviewed until January 1967.

The *Book Review Digest* is most helpful in determining the initial critical reactions to a book, especially if you wish to compare the immediate responses of sophisticated readers with judgments made by scholars and critics after the work had had a chance to influence other writers or after public tastes had changed. Examples of research assignments requiring you to locate such information would be "Initial Critical Reactions to Ernest Hemingway's *The Sun Also Rises,*" and "Changing Critical Evaluations of Willa Cather's *My Antonia.*"

Use of the *Book Review Digest* is not limited to literary topics. For example, you might want to know how reviewers reacted to a book that presented a new view of a well-known person or event or that unveiled a new social or scientific theory, such as evolution, relativity, or psychoanalysis.

Finally, if a book you want to use as a source appears in the *Book Review Digest,* you can find out very easily whether the reviewers thought that book informative and reliable.

Indexes to Scholarly and Professional Journals

THE HUMANITIES INDEX AND THE SOCIAL SCIENCES INDEX

These indexes may well provide you, at least as an undergraduate, with all the sources you will need for research papers in the social sciences and the humanities. These indexes are more specialized than those discussed so far, and each indexes not general magazines but scholarly journals in a variety of fields.

Since 1974 the *Humanities Index* and *Social Sciences Index* have appeared as separate volumes. From 1965 to 1974 the two indexes were combined in the *Social Sciences and Humanities Index,* and from 1920 to 1965 its title was the *International Index to Periodicals.* From 1907 through 1919 the single index was titled *Readers' Guide Supplement and International Index.*

Together, the *Humanities Index* and the *Social Sciences Index* cover articles published in more than five hundred scholarly and professional journals. (Many of these journals, however, are not carried by small libraries.) The *Humanities Index* lists articles according to subject in the following academic disciplines "and related subjects":

archaeology	literary and political criticism
classical studies	performing arts
area studies	philosophy
folklore	religion
history (not included until 1974)	theology
language and literature	

The *Social Sciences Index* lists articles according to subject in the following academic disciplines "and related subjects":

anthropology	medical science
area studies	political sciences
economics	psychology (not included between
environmental science	1945 and 1974)
education	public administration
law and criminology	sociology

SPECIALIZED INDEXES

The *Humanities Index* and the *Social Sciences Index,* though highly valuable resources, cover only a small fraction of all the scholarly and professional journals published in the humanities and the social sciences, and of course none of those devoted to the natural and applied sciences. Because the number of specialized scholarly articles published each year is enormous, each field has its own annual index to specialized periodicals within that field. Some fields, such as English literature, cannot be contained within a single annual index, so there are still more specialized indexes.

These indexes, and the articles they list, will lead you to very difficult materials. Most authors of scholarly articles are writing for fellow experts and therefore assume that their readers have a strong background in the field; many articles focus on very narrow topics and employ a highly specialized terminology. You may therefore find much scholarly writing hard to understand and harder still to use in your own research project. Later in college, especially in your major field, the information in scholarly journals will become increasingly valuable to you. For now, you may want your instructor's advice as to whether looking up such articles will be worth your while.

At the end of this chapter is a selective list of indexes to scholarly and professional journals in many major fields. If you need to find additional sources, consult the *Bibliographic Index: A Cumulative Bibliography of Bibliographies*. This work briefly describes all the periodical indexes you will probably ever need.

Locating Periodicals

Most libraries have a periodical room where you can find the current issue of each magazine and newspaper to which the library subscribes. Most of your research, however, will involve back (previous) issues, and these may be kept elsewhere.

Libraries usually have back issues of periodical magazines and journals gathered by year—or, if the periodical is published very often or is bulky, into shorter periods—and permanently rebound in hard covers. These bound volumes are then shelved chronologically, either in the periodical room or in the stacks. Back issues that are not in the periodical room may be in the library offices awaiting rebinding or actually at the bindery; ask a librarian for any such issues you need to work with.

Back issues of daily and weekly newspapers are kept unbound for one or more years. Then, in many libraries, they are thrown away. However, the Sunday magazine and book review sections may be kept much longer and may be bound for permanent storage. A librarian at your library can tell you what its policy is.

Additional Resources

Although you can produce a fine research paper based entirely on books and periodicals found through the card catalog and the major periodical indexes, there are other resources both in the library and outside it where you may find still more information and ideas.

IN THE LIBRARY

Specialized Collections. Some libraries maintain separate collections of materials such as books, periodicals, personal letters, and manuscripts. A special collection sometimes relates to special areas of interest: a particular author's works, the history of a particular place, or a fairly narrow field (cave exploration, Broadway musicals, or aviation engineering). Other special collections are kept separate from the main collection because their holdings are fragile, rare, or otherwise unusual. The catalog for each special collection is usually separate and kept in a designated section of the library.

Microforms. To save space and increase usefulness, many source materials have been preserved on microforms, mainly microfilm or microfiche. The most common resources on microforms are periodicals, and others include old and rare books and even facsimiles of manuscripts. Some sources, such as graduate dissertations, may be published only on microforms. A microfilm comes in the form of a reel of film with one or two pages per frame. A microfiche is a card-shaped piece of film containing up to 100 printed pages, greatly reduced. Reading either requires the use of a special viewer, usually kept in a separate room or area in the library.

Vertical File Index. Some printed sources may not be classified either as books or as periodicals, and so will not appear in either the card catalog or the periodical indexes. Such materials include pamphlets, brochures, and clippings from hard-to-get periodicals on specialized topics. You can find these resources by using the Vertical File Index. A librarian can explain how to use this index.

Audiovisual Materials. Many libraries now contain media sections which house films, videotapes, pictures, slides, and sound recordings. If your topic concerns the performing or visual arts, or architecture, you will often find materials useful to your research in the audiovisual collection. You may also find documentaries in the social and natural sciences, especially in those fields having to do with human and animal behavior and society.

Interlibrary Loan. If you discover a source which you believe to be crucial to your research, and your library does not have a copy of it, you may be able to borrow the source through an interlibrary loan arranged by a librarian. (**Warning:** It normally takes several weeks for the source to arrive at your library, and it may take longer. Allow sufficient time for the loan to be arranged.)

OUTSIDE THE LIBRARY

Other Libraries. Large colleges and universities may have separate, specialized libraries attached to particular graduate schools or departments, such as law, medicine, engineering, music, and art. Off campus, museums and professional societies devoted to such fields often operate their own small but excellent libraries. You may have to apply formally to use such facilities; often simply verifying your school affiliation will be enough. The public library in your city may also be a useful resource. Some, like the New York Public Library, are among the greatest research facilities in the world, but even the most modest public library may have the particular periodical or book you need.

Special Printed Materials. Private businesses, nonprofit organizations, special interest groups, and various levels of government publish reports and pamphlets in great numbers. Usually these materials can be obtained free of charge by writing to the organizations. In most cases there will be no catalog to which you can refer, so you may be able only to describe what you are looking for and hope the answer meets your needs. The United States Government Printing Office *Monthly Catalog* lists all publications by the federal government that are available to the public, their prices, and the addresses from which they may be ordered. Your library should have a copy, and you can ask your librarian where it is kept. Be warned, however, that delivery is not overnight: the GPO distribution center in Pueblo, Colorado, alone handles some 80,000 requests every week, and you may wait a month or more for materials ordered.

Television and Radio Programs. The Public Broadcasting System (PBS) regularly presents documentaries about the performing and graphic arts and also the natural and social sciences. These programs are often repeated periodically, so that you may be able to watch broadcasts originally shown before you started your research project. If your topic has to do with a current issue, interviews and documentaries may be scheduled on any station. Transcripts of regularly scheduled news interviews are often available from the stations or networks that produce or broadcast them. Because transcripts usually require four to six weeks' delivery time, you will in most cases have to make your own transcription. If possible, record the program and later transcribe those portions of it you want to use word by word, rather than trying to take notes during the program.

Letters and Interviews. You may want to set up an interview of your own with a person whose knowledge or opinions would be useful to your project. Perhaps a faculty member is an authority on your topic, or a local public official or civil servant is responsible for running a program that is relevant to your research. When you request a personal interview, specify your field of inquiry as precisely as you can, and write down your questions before going to the interview. You may even want to send your questions in advance, so that the authority will be able to consider his or her answers. Finally, limit the interview to a period of time agreeable to the interviewee and yourself.

More often you will have to ask your questions by letter and hope that the authority has the time and inclination to answer you. Again, limit yourself to a few carefully phrased questions. Your chances of getting an answer will be that much greater.

Questionnaires and Surveys. If your topic involves public opinion, particularly the opinions of a particular group such as college students or faculty, the parents of school children, or senior citizens, you may find that no poll has been published that serves your purposes and decide to conduct a poll of your own. Whether you conduct your survey in person or by mail through questionnaires, your questions must be carefully stated to make sure that the answers are relevant and meaningful. You should probably ask your instructor to review your list of questions before you begin your poll.

Some General Bibliographies, Periodical Indexes, and Representative Journals

Here are some guides to sources which you will find in many college libraries and which you can use to develop your working bibliography. Also consult the bibliographies that accompany articles in the general reference books you use for background reading.

ART AND ARCHITECTURE

Art Index, The: A Cumulative Author and Subject Index to a Selected List of Fine Art Periodicals. New York: H. W. Wilson, 1933–present. (Quarterly, with biennial cumulations.) In addition to fine arts, index includes architecture, design, and decorating journals.

ASTRONOMY

Sky and Telescope. Cambridge, Mass.: Sky Publishing, 1941–present. (Monthly.) Publication for non-specialists in astronomy: articles, observations, data, equipment guides, etc.

BIOGRAPHY

Biography Index, The: A Cumulative Index to Biographical Material in Books and Magazines. New York: H. W. Wilson, 1947–present. (Quarterly, with annual and triennial cumulations.)

BIOLOGY

Biological Abstracts. Philadelphia: Biosciences Information Service, 1926–present. (Bimonthly.) Abstracts and index of international publications, excludes clinical medicine.

BUSINESS

Business Periodicals Index. New York: H. W. Wilson, 1958–present. (Monthly, except July.)

CHEMISTRY

Chemical Abstracts. Easton, Pa.: American Chemical Society, 1907–present. (Weekly.)

DRAMA

Breed, Paul F., and Florence M. Sniderman. *Dramatic Criticism Index: A Bibliography of Commentaries on Playwrights from Ibsen to the Avant-Garde.* Detroit: Gale, 1972.

Cumulated Dramatic Index, 1909–40. A Cumulation of the F. W. Faxon Company's Dramatic Index. Ed. Frederick W. Faxon, et al. 2 vols. Boston: G. K. Hall, 1965.

Play Index. New York: H. W. Wilson, 1953–78. 5 vols.

ECONOMICS

American Journal of Economics and Sociology. New York: American Journal of
Economics and Sociology, 1941–present. (Quarterly.)

Hughes, Catherine, ed. *Economic Education: A Guide to Information Sources.*
Detroit: Gale, 1977.

International Bibliography of Economics. Ed. UNESCO International Committee
for Social Science Documentation. Chicago: Aldine, 1952–present. (Annual.)

EDUCATION

Current Index to Journals in Education. Phoenix, Ariz.: Oryx Press, 1969–present.
(Monthly, with annual and semiannual cumulations.)

Education Index, The. New York: H. W. Wilson, 1929–present. (Monthly, except
July and August, with annual cumulations.)

ENGINEERING

Applied Science and Technology Index. New York: H. W. Wilson, 1958–present.
(Monthly.)

Engineering Index, The. Ed. American Society of Mechanical Engineers. New
York: Engineering Index, 1920–present. (Monthly.)

Malinowsky, Harold R., et al. *Science and Engineering Literature: A Guide to
Reference Sources.* 2nd ed. Littleton, Colo.: Libraries Unlimited, 1976.

ENVIRONMENTAL SCIENCE

Pollution Abstracts. Ed. Oceanic Library and Information Center. Louisville,
Ky.: Data Courier, 1970–present.

ETHNIC STUDIES

Index to Literature on the American Indian. San Francisco: Indian Historian Press,
1970–present. (Annual.)

Index to Periodical Articles by and about Negroes. Ed. Hallie Q. Brown Memorial
Library. Boston: G. K. Hall, 1950–present. (Annual.)

Welsch, Ervin K. *The Negro in the United States: A Research Guide.* Bloomington:
Indiana University Press, 1965. Discusses books and periodicals.

HEALTH AND PHYSICAL EDUCATION

American Alliance for Health, Physical Education and Recreation. *Abstracts of
Research Papers.* Washington, D.C.: AAHPER, 1971–1975.

HISTORY

America: History and Life. A Guide to Periodical Literature. Santa Barbara, Calif.: American Bibliographical Center, Clio Press, 1964–present. (Annual.)

American Historical Association. *Guide to Historical Literature.* Ed. George F. Howe et al. New York: Macmillan, 1961.

Guide to the Study of the United States of America, A: Representative Books Reflecting the Development of American Thought. Washington, D.C.: U.S. Government Printing Office, 1960. Supplements 1956–1965, 1976.

Historical Abstracts: Bibliography of the World's Periodical Literature, 1775–. Santa Barbara, Calif.: American Bibliographical Center, Clio Press, 1955–present. (Annual.)

International Bibliography of Historical Sciences. New York: International Publications Service, 1930–present. (Annual.)

LANGUAGE AND LITERATURE

Bond, Donald F. *Reference Guide to English Studies.* 2nd ed. Chicago: University of Chicago Press, 1971.

Essay and General Literature Index 1900–1933: An Index to about 40,000 Essays and Articles in 2,144 Volumes of Collections of Essays and Miscellaneous Works. New York: H. W. Wilson, 1934–present. (Biennial supplements.)

Kennedy, Arthur G., and Donald B. Sands. *Concise Bibliography for Students of English, A.* 5th ed. Rev. William E. Coburn. Stanford: Stanford University Press, 1972.

Modern Humanities Research Association. *Annual Bibliography of English Language and Literature.* Cambridge: Cambridge University Press, 1921–present.

Modern Language Association of America. *MLA International Bibliography of Books and Articles on the Modern Languages and Literature.* New York: MLA. 1922–1968 as June issue of *PMLA.* (Formerly *American Bibliography.*) 1969–present.

New Cambridge Bibliography of English Literature, The. New York: Cambridge University Press, 1969–77. 5 vols.

Spiller, Robert E., et al. *The Literary History of the United States.* 4th ed. 2 vols. New York: Macmillan, 1974.

LAW

Index to Legal Periodicals. New York: H. W. Wilson for the American Association of Law Libraries, 1908–present. (Monthly.)

MUSIC

Duckles, Vincent, *Music Reference and Research Materials: An Annotated Bibliography.* 2nd ed. New York: Macmillan, 1974.

Music Index: The Key to Current Music Periodical Literature. Detroit: Information Service, 1949–present. (Monthly, with annual cumulations.)

RILM Abstracts. New York: International Association of Music Libraries, 1967–present. (Quarterly.)

PHILOSOPHY

Philosopher's Index, The: An International Index to Philosophical Periodicals. Bowling Green, Ohio: Bowling Green University, 1967–present. (Quarterly.)

PHYSICS

Science Abstracts. London: Institution of Electrical Engineers, 1898–present. (Monthly.) Includes abstracts of articles about physics.

POLITICAL SCIENCE

Brock, Clifton. *The Literature of Political Science: A Guide for Students, Librarians, and Teachers.* New York: Bowker, 1969.

Harmon, Robert B. *Political Science: A Bibliographic Guide to the Literature.* Metuchen, N.J.: Scarecrow, 1965. Third Supplement, 1974.

PSYCHOLOGY

Harvard List of Books in Psychology, The. 4th ed. Cambridge, Mass.: Harvard University Press, 1971.

Psychological Abstracts. Washington, D.C.: American Psychological Association, 1927–present. (Monthly.)

RELIGION

American Theological Library Association. *Index to Religious Periodical Literature, 1949/1952–.* Chicago: American Theological Library Association, 1953–present. (Annual.)

Religious and Theological Abstracts. Youngstown, Ohio: Theological Publishers, 1958–present. (Quarterly.)

SOCIOLOGY

Social Sciences Index. New York: H. W. Wilson, 1965–present. (Quarterly.) See p. 46 of this book for a complete description.

White, Carl M., et al. *Sources of Information in the Social Sciences: A Guide to the Literature.* 3rd ed. Chicago: American Library Association, 1973.

WOMEN

Backscheider, Paula R., and Felicity A. Backscheider. *An Annotated Bibliography of 20th Century Critical Studies of Women and Literature, 1660–1800.* New York: Garland, 1977.

Krichman, Albert. *The Women's Rights Movement in the United States, 1848–1970: A Bibliography and Sourcebook.* Metuchen, N.J.: Scarecrow, 1972.

Review Questions

1. Suppose you are looking for a biography of Queen Elizabeth I of England called *Elizabeth the First* by Paul Johnson. How many entries in the card catalog can you find for this book? How can the card catalog help you locate other books about Queen Elizabeth?

2. How is each of these pieces of information, found on cards in the card catalog, useful to researchers?

   author   date of publication
   title   number of pages
   subject   notation about a
   call number   bibliography

3. What kinds of materials are listed in periodical indexes? Why might a researcher need to use several different indexes?

4. For each of the following topics, what additional resources (besides books from the card catalog and periodical articles from indexes) might you look for?

   - the latest government recommendations about energy conservation
   - a seventeenth-century book (all known copies are owned by British libraries)
   - the inauguration address of President Kennedy
   - the jobs located by recent graduates of your school
   - the history of the town in which your library is located
   - your city's model program for rat control
   - the major paintings of a particular artist
   - the position on a controversial issue taken last week by the governor

Exercises

1. Just to feel more at home in your school library, pay a visit there and locate the following:

- the reference room or reference area
- the periodical room or area
- the reserve reading room or reserve desk
- the card catalog

   If your library provides a diagram or floor plan of its physical layout, obtain a copy and use it to locate these resources. If no diagram is available, draw a rough floor plan of your own, showing the locations of the main sections of the library.

2. Use the card catalog to look up a fairly recent work of fiction by a well-known author, perhaps one you have studied in high school or college. Consult your library's classification guide to find the shelf where the book should be located. Use the *Book Review Digest* to find out if the book was reviewed during the year it was published or the following year. Report your findings.

3. Using microfilms of the *New York Times*, find the most important story reported on the day and year you were born (the "lead" story is in the upper right-hand corner of the front page). Then go to the *New York Times Index*, find a listing for this article and the next *Times* article on the same subject. Copy out both listings and convert all abbreviations to the full forms of the words that they represent.

4. Use the *Readers' Guide to Periodical Literature* to locate in your library an article published during the past year about your favorite hobby, pastime, or field of interest. Read it, determine the author's topic and thesis, and explain briefly why you agree or disagree with this thesis.

5. Choose one of the topics listed on page 00 of this book. Use the subject card catalog to try to find the titles of three books related to the topic. Write out these titles and their call numbers and describe briefly where in the library each is located.

6. Think of a topic in psychology or medical science that interests you. Use the *Social Science Index* to discover how many articles have been written on that topic during the past three years. Record appropriate article and journal titles and any other information provided in the index description. Convert all abbreviations to the full forms of the words that they represent.

4

Searching for Sources

Now that you have a good idea of the research aids available in your library, you can begin the process of searching for sources by developing a *working bibliography*—a list of the books and periodical articles that may become sources of information for your research paper. Once you have collected a substantial list of possible sources, you must locate as many of them as you can and examine each one briefly to see whether it contains information and ideas that will further the investigation of your specific topic. Ultimately, you will use some of the information you find in these sources to support your paper's thesis. Those sources that provide specific ideas and information for the paper will be listed in your *final bibliography*.

Compiling the Working Bibliography

To begin putting together a working bibliography, get a supply of three- by five-inch note cards for *bibliography cards*. Then, whenever you come across the title of a book or article that seems worth checking into, make out a bibliography card for it. Use a separate card for each item and keep the cards in alphabetical order. Cards are handier for this purpose than a simple list because they can more easily be kept in order as you add and drop items from your working bibliography.

THE INFORMATION ON BIBLIOGRAPHY CARDS

For a bibliography card to be useful, it must contain all the information you will need when you prepare the footnotes or endnotes and the bibliography for your paper. In addition, the card should give you whatever information is needed to find the book or article in the library.

To make out a card for a book, record the following information in the order given below (see Figure 4–1):

- name(s) of the author(s),
- title of the book, underlined
- place of publication
- publisher's name
- date of publication

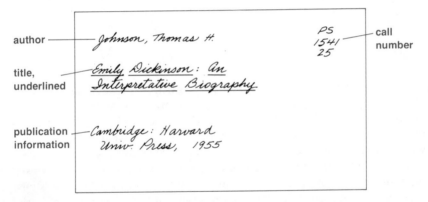

author

title, underlined

publication information

PS
1541
25

call number

Johnson, Thomas H.

Emily Dickinson: An
Interpretative Biography

Cambridge: Harvard
Univ. Press, 1955

Figure 4–1. Bibliography card for a book

For a periodical article, follow this guide (see Figure 4–2):

- name(s) of the author(s)
- title of the article, in quotation marks
- title of the periodical, underlined
- volume number and date of publication
- numbers of the pages on which the article appears

Be sure to place in the upper right corner of every bibliography card the library call number or other "locator" information from the card catalog. Take extra care to copy all bibliographical information accu-

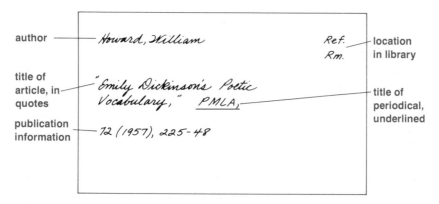

Figure 4–2. Bibliography card for a periodical article

rately onto your cards. Misspellings, incorrect punctuation, careless omissions, and other mistakes in copying can force you to waste time in return trips to the library.

Gathering Sources

You will almost always accumulate more sources for your working bibliography than you end up listing in your final bibliography. This happens because many of the titles you come across will, upon close examination, prove to be of little or no help in the investigation of your hypothesis. Also, since the hypothesis may change as you progress in your research, sources that once seemed useful may have to be discarded. Therefore, you can expect to add and drop titles from the working bibliography throughout the research project.

STRATEGIES FOR GATHERING SOURCES

You should begin assembling a working bibliography while taking notes during your background reading. The student who wrote about Jefferson Davis came across several potentially useful titles at the end of the encyclopedia article on "Davis." He then went to the card catalog to learn whether those titles were available in his library. Four of them were, and three of these items yielded information that directly supported his eventual thesis. Furthermore, these three books also contained bibliographies which, in turn, led to other useful sources. In this way, the student was able to acquire a sizable working bibliography before he began a methodical search through the card catalog for promising titles.

Once he had followed up these early leads, the student moved to the card catalog. He looked under subject headings that were obviously related to his topic, such as "Davis, Jefferson, 1808–1889" and "U.S.—History—Civil War 1861–1865." Next, he used several cross-reference cards to find other headings that were not so obvious.

He rejected many items—such as A. H. Abel's *The American Indian as Participant in the Civil War*—without further examination because their titles indicated they were virtually certain to say nothing of value on his topic. He did make out bibliography cards for the many titles that seemed at all likely to prove useful. Later, when he examined each of these items one at a time, he eliminated most of them from his working bibliography because they turned out to be either popular accounts or survey studies, such as textbooks, which repeated the same general information about Davis and his problems as president.

Finally, George Pitman searched through several periodical indexes, starting with the latest volume and going back about a dozen years. A fair number of articles listed under "Davis" and related Civil War headings had appeared in periodicals to which his college library subscribed. Again, the titles of some articles clearly indicated that they bore little or no relevance to his particular topic, and so he left them out of his working bibliography. Several others he recorded on cards, but they, too, were eventually rejected as sources either because they did not relate directly to the topic or because he had already found the information they contained in books. (Referring to these last articles would have resulted in a needless repetition of ideas and added nothing to the paper.) As it turned out, George Pitman used only one periodical article as a source for his paper—one that he had found in the bibliography accompanying an article he did not use. That one article, however, became extremely valuable because it provided strong evidence of Davis's moral strength.

As you can see, this student employed a number of strategies when searching for sources. Although most of the evidence for his paper was destined to be found in books rather than periodicals, he could not know this in advance. He had to discover it for himself through conscientious research.

The student who researched Emily Dickinson used the same basic strategies for gathering sources but with somewhat different results. Her final bibliography lists several books about Dickinson's life and works, two periodical articles, an essay from a collection of literary criticism, two volumes of the poet's works, and a collection of the poet's letters. Along the way, she found and skimmed numerous other books and articles, but these turned out to be mainly analyses of Dickinson's poems, without useful references to her life.

The search for sources is a journey into the unknown that tests your imagination, perseverance, and ability to plan. Sometimes this search can be frustrating because many clues lead nowhere and seem to waste your time. But do not try to save time by hastily rejecting items whose titles do not indicate a clear and immediate relation to your topic. Ambiguous clues must always be followed up. The possible source that is discarded unseen may be the very one you need the most.

Reassessing Your Topic

Once you have compiled a working bibliography for your project, you should pause to consider whether your topic still seems workable or whether it is too broad or too narrow. A topic that is too broad requires you to read more sources and write a longer paper than your time allows. You must determine at this point whether you have sufficient time to complete all the work necessary for a good research paper. If your schedule is tight, you might do well to restrict your topic further. Be careful, however, not to narrow your topic to the extent that it can be adequately researched from a very small number of sources. Conversely, if your working bibliography is small and the prospect of finding additional sources is slight, you must prepare to expand your topic.

The first of the sample papers in Chapter 9 was developed from ten sources, the second from twelve. In general, a research paper is expected to use from five to twenty sources. Because a working bibliography is likely to contain titles which, upon examination, prove irrelevant to the topic or duplicate information found in other sources, your working bibliography should include no fewer than ten titles, or your topic may well be too narrow. On the other hand, if it includes over forty titles, your topic is probably too broad.

IF THE TOPIC IS TOO NARROW

If you find your topic is too narrow, do not discard all your preliminary research and start again from scratch. In all likelihood, you can find a way to expand its range to embrace a broader issue or more information requiring your analysis. To broaden a topic in a field with which you are not altogether familiar, you will probably have to return to your background sources. In the case of a narrow topic mentioned earlier—*how the ozone layer protects the earth from deadly radiation*—further background reading might disclose that scientists are worried that the ozone layer may be damaged or destroyed by fluorocarbons, substances used to spray deodorants and similar materials from aerosol cans. Although there is broad scientific agreement that fluorocarbons can break down ozone, scientists do not agree on the danger from consumer products such as hairspray and shaving cream. You might therefore shift to a broader related topic, *the effect of fluorocarbons on the ozone layer*, and form a new hypothesis: "Fluorocarbon propellants in aerosol cans pose a serious danger to the ozone layer." The entries already in your working bibliography might help in describing the composition and function of the ozone layer, and you would now look for sources that support or oppose your hypothesis.

IF THE TOPIC IS TOO BROAD

We have already seen how George Pitman narrowed a very broad topic—*Jefferson Davis*—to the manageable *Jefferson Davis's performance as president of the Confederacy.* Pitman was able to narrow his topic before starting his search for sources, but another less fortunate student had to stop and change her topic long after she had begun compiling her working bibliography.

This sudent had chosen to write on the topic *schizophrenia,* which seemed manageable at first. The psychology textbook she used for her background reading assigned only four pages to the topic and included only a brief bibliography on schizophrenia at the end of the chapter. What she did not know, but later found out, was that her college library contained many books and hundreds of articles exclusively about schizophrenia. As she was preparing her thirtieth bibliography card, she realized that there were probably ten times as many possible scources for this topic yet to be recorded. To limit her topic, she looked through her stack of bibliography cards, hoping to find a narrower topic that was still broad enough to justify research.

She noticed that several of the titles mentioned the *nature of schizophrenia,* others its *causes,* others its *effect on those living with schizophrenics,* and still others its *treatment.* She remembered from her background reading that doctors use several different methods of treatment because of uncertainty regarding the causes of the disorder. Although she was interested in the treatment of schizophrenia, she realized from looking at her working bibliography that this, too, was likely to prove too broad for her paper. So she reviewed her background reading notes once more and decided to narrow her topic still further, to one kind of treatment. Her new topic became *treatment of schizophrenia in a community setting.* She also needed to form a new hypothesis and decided on "Treating schizophrenia in a community setting is a new idea that works."

In making out a new working bibliography, the student began with titles from the old one. But something seemed wrong. She could not eliminate very many of the thirty titles in her working bibliography because any book on schizophrenia might refer to the type of treatment she was investigating. Even if it did not, it might help demonstrate that the method works. Clearly, her hypothesis needed to be revised again, this time to give it sharper focus. Reviewing those background notes that mentioned the new method of treatment, she saw that it was applied only to severe cases. And its proponents did not claim success in all cases, only better results than treatment in institutions. This led her to recast her hypothesis again: "Treating severe schizophrenia in a community setting has in some cases proven more successful than treatment in traditional institutions."

The sharper focus provided by the revised hypothesis saved the student from reading and taking notes on matters that were not directly related to her purposes, such as treatment outside of mental institutions (but not in community settings), the history of treating schizophrenia, or the treatment of mild schizophrenia.

Let's compare the two hypotheses. The first contains only two terms that give any focus to the topic—*new idea* and *works*. *New idea* refers to a minor point that can be made simply by giving the date of the first use of this method. *Works* gives some focus, but it is rather vague, lacking the sense of scientific validity carried by "has proven more successful." In contrast, the second hypothesis has four key terms— *severe, proven, successful,* and *traditional institutions*—that helped the student to search for sources and read them far more efficiently. *Severe* warned her to avoid reading about milder forms of the disorder which do not force sufferers to be committed to mental hospitals. *Proven* kept her attention focused on the need to find specific evidence for or against her hypothesis. The term *successful* made her consider a valid basis for judging success—a difficult problem in this situation because schizophrenia is rarely, if ever, cured; the sufferer's symptoms only become less distressing. The student had to look closely to find the criteria used by her various sources in order to determine how much improvement could reasonably be considered "success." *Traditional institutions* reminded her that if she wanted to show that this method is successful, she had to compare it with well-established treatments, rather than with other experimental approaches.

Skimming Your Sources

When you are satisfied that your topic is workable and you have compiled an adequate working bibliography, you are almost ready to begin the close reading and thorough note-taking that lie at the heart of the research process. Before you begin that challenging work, however, you need to be sure that your working bibliography will be adequate for your purposes. You can find this out by skimming all the potential sources before beginning to read them closely.

The purpose of skimming is to decide quickly whether each source is likely to further your investigation by providing information and ideas relevant to your hypothesis. Essentially, you skim to eliminate unhelpful sources and to get an idea of how the remaining sources will be useful to you. If, after skimming, you have cut your working bibliography down to five or fewer titles, you may have to find a broader topic. If your skimming leaves you with more than twenty fairly substantial sources to read, and you do not have time to do that much reading, you may have to narrow your topic.

SKIMMING BOOKS

Skimming a book begins with the table of contents and the index. The table of contents usually presents a broad outline of the book's organization. If the author discusses your particular topic, you may be able to find out from the chapter titles how extensive the discussion is and what major points it raises. Briefer discussions within chapters can be found by using the index. The index gives page numbers for each reference to your topic, however brief they may be.

When you are using an index, take the time to check all the headings that might be relevant to your topic, not just the obvious ones. For example, if your topic were *reading problems of grade-school boys as opposed to those of grade-school girls* (in this age group boys with reading trouble outnumber girls by a ratio of four to one), you would naturally look in a book's index under *reading, grade-school,* and *boys.* Some references would probably be listed under *reading,* but the other two terms might not appear in the index. In that case, you could look under synonyms for these terms, such as *elementary school* and "male." Do not stop at synonyms, however. Think of different ways to approach the topic which might lead you to other, possibly more fruitful headings, such as *learning disabilities* or *disabilities, learning* and *sex as a factor in learning.*

Finally, if you feel certain that a particular book is important to your research, but you have trouble finding what you want, do not give up. Instead, go through the index item by item, searching for significant headings that may not have occurred to you.

When you locate in a book passages that deal with your topic, skim the first line or two of each paragraph. In this way, you are likely to discover the author's main points, which are often stated in topic sentences. In addition, if the book has chapter summaries, read those that pertain to your topic.

SKIMMING PERIODICAL ARTICLES

Articles seldom have their own tables of contents, and so you will probably have to skim the first line of each paragraph throughout an article to see whether it includes anything useful to you. An article may, however, include an abstract that summarizes its thesis and major supporting points. If the abstract indicates that the article might be worth reading, you need not skim. If, on the other hand, the abstract does not mention material that is likely to help you, do not drop the source from your working bibliography. Because abstracts are concise, they may omit significant details that might be useful to your project. These details you would find by skimming.

When skimming a possible source, take notes that tell you how the source might be useful or why it is of no use. Put these notes on the bibliography card for the source in question.

In order to determine whether a source is likely to help you, skim with the following questions in mind:

- Is this item relevant to your topic?
- How extensive is the discussion of your topic?
- Does this item support or contradict your hypothesis?

Avoid taking detailed notes at this time; simply summarize the usefulness of the possible source insofar as your project is concerned.

Always keep a record of the sources you evaluate. Do not discard the bibliography cards for those sources you decide not to use. If you later decide to broaden or narrow your topic, of if you later modify your hypothesis, the same sources which first seemed irrelevant may suddenly become very important. You will save considerable time if you do not have to retrieve information about a source you have previously skimmed.

Evaluating Potential Sources

As you skim through potential sources, you are evaluating each one of them in terms of its later usefulness to you. Here are some further suggestions for making this evaluation.

THE EXTENT OF COVERAGE

Not every book or article that deals directly with your topic will be valuable as a source for your paper. In general, any source that treats your topic extensively will be more useful than a source that covers it superficially. You are looking for sources that give you a deeper, more detailed understanding of some aspect of your topic and thus help you to judge the accuracy of your hypothesis.

For example, almost all books on the Civil War at least mention Jefferson Davis, and many of them sum up his performance as president in a paragraph or two. These short commentaries are usually too general to be useful as sources; the information they give is boiled down from more detailed studies, and it is the latter that you should be looking for. Any writer can state with some justification that Davis was "an ineffective president because he did not always work well with other Southern leaders," and such sweeping generalizations may not necessarily be wrong. In a research paper, however, you are expected to go beyond mere generalization and find specific examples, in this case of Davis's troubles with those other leaders. Otherwise neither you nor your readers will have a basis for deciding whether your conclusion is well supported.

If several potential sources offer exactly the same factual information on your topic, you need not read all of them closely. Choose one source to represent the group, and take notes on it. This approach, however, should not be used when several sources draw the same general conclusion from the basic facts. All such judgments should be mentioned in your paper. The difference here is purely in the kind of material repeated in the several sources: although "facts" (the number of Emily Dickinson's poems published during her life) are occasionally open to question, you are primarily interested in the importance that prominent scholars have attached to the available evidence.

THE NEED FOR A VARIETY OF VIEWPOINTS

While putting together your working bibliography, remember to include works written by different experts in the field. A paper that depends mainly on the opinions and interpretations of one writer might well be criticized for that very reason. For example, look at this list of books that a student believed sufficient for the paper being written.

Topic: *Lee and Grant: the old vs. the new style of warfare*

Hypothesis: "The South's initial military success was due in large part to Robert E. Lee's mastery of the limited forms of warfare that characterized the early years of the Civil War, but the tide of battle turned when Lee was unable to cope with Ulysses S. Grant's new strategy of total war."

Sources:
1. *Glory Road*, Bruce Catton
2. *Grant Moves South*, Bruce Catton
3. *Grant Takes Command*, Bruce Catton
4. *Mr. Lincoln's Army*, Bruce Catton
5. *The Civil War*, Bruce Catton
6. *Robert E. Lee*, Douglas Freeman
7. *Lincoln Finds a General*, K. P. Williams

This bibliography is so heavily weighted with Catton's works that his views are almost certain to dominate a paper based on these sources. An alert researcher would notice this imbalance and take steps to remedy the situation. Maybe some of Catton's books could be dropped if they largely repeated each other in regard to this topic. In any event, other authorities' works must be found in order to support or oppose Catton's views.

One further question about balance comes to mind when looking over this list of titles. Isn't something wrong when four of the sources deal with Grant while just one focuses on Lee? After all, the topic suggests equal treatment of the two.

THE PROBLEM OF OBSOLESCENCE

Another important factor to keep in mind when evaluating sources is that some are almost certain to be out of date. Especially in the natural and social sciences, knowledge is increasing so rapidly that theories, and even facts, may often be revised or discarded within as little as three to five years. Even history may be rewritten when new evidence comes to light or when historians devise new ways to look at the past.

Some historical topics require you to find contemporary sources. If you were to write about Senator Joseph McCarthy's impact as a communist-hunter during the early 1950s, you would read newspaper and magazine stories and editorials of the time in addition to current evaluations of that period. If you intended to find out how Winston Churchill's wartime speeches affected the morale of the English people, you would consult letters, memoirs, and again newspapers and magazines of the early 1940s for the most vivid evidence—evidence that might well contradict some current historical opinions. Literary scholars are often interested in how famous writers and their works were received when they were new; such questions can only be answered by research into old sources.

If your topic requires you to know about the latest findings and opinions—and most topics do—the newest sources will usually be the most relevant as well. If you decide that an older source may still be worth close reading, make sure that you examine more recent sources first so that you will have some sense of what information in the older source has become obsolete.

PRIMARY AND SECONDARY SOURCES

Many researchers divide their sources into those which are primary and those which are secondary. The difference between the two is important but not always easy to keep clear. A primary source is the original product of a writer's experience, observation, and mind, reproduced in the writer's own words. Secondary sources, on the other hand, are those which use or comment on primary sources. For example, in the bibliography for Susanna Andrews's paper on Emily Dickinson, only three sources—the two collections of Dickinson's poems and the collection of her letters—are primary, while the other nine sources are secondary.

What makes the distinction between primary and secondary sources tricky is that a single source may be secondary for one researcher and primary for another, depending on their topics. For example, Yvor Winters's essay, "Emily Dickinson and the Limits of Judgment," is a secondary source for any writer about Emily Dickinson, because it is someone else's interpretation of Dickinson, not the poet speaking for herself. On the other hand, for research about Yvor Winters himself, his essay would be a primary source since it presents Winters's observations and thoughts on a particular subject (Emily Dickinson) in his own words.

A primary source is not necessarily more reliable than a secondary source which comments on it. Certain historical figures have written memoirs and given speeches and interviews which were designed to hide the truth or to distort it in ways favorable to themselves; and even honest witnesses may observe and remember events differently. Still, whenever you can, you should try to identify the primary sources for your topic and consult them if possible. Even if they later turn out to be the writings of a liar, a villain, or a fool, your impressions will be firsthand, not filtered through a secondary source.

ARTICLES IN POPULAR PERIODICALS

When looking for sources you will often find references to articles in newspapers and in popular magazines such as *Time, Newsweek, Business Week, Psychology Today, Atlantic Monthly, Reader's Digest,* or *Cosmopolitan.* Such sources are usually distinguished from specialized journals, such as *Science, Nature, PMLA, English Studies, Foreign Affairs, American Historical Review, Yale Law Journal,* or the *Journal of Social Psychology.* The distinction has less to do with subject matter and frequency of publication than with understandable differences in quality between magazine information and journal information.

Articles in journals are carefully prepared, documented, and edited to ensure that the information they contain is authoritative—or at least accurate, given what is known at the time. This cannot always be said for articles in magazines because the decision to publish an article is often based on current interest in its subject matter. As a result, such articles may distort complex or highly technical matters in an effort to make them easy to understand. Some popular magazines sensationalize events in order to heighten their appeal, and others slant their accounts of events to cater to political or other biases of their particular readership. Furthermore, newspapers and magazines that strive to keep abreast of the news often require their writers to produce articles on very tight schedules, leaving them little time to analyze or even verify information before rushing into print. Even guest articles written by distinguished authorities may lack accuracy and detail because such experts also try to popularize their subjects for a general audience. For all these reasons, you should be wary when using magazines as sources for a paper. For a topic such as "Henry Kissinger's efforts to settle the Mideast crisis," a *Cosmopolitan* interview with Kissinger in 1973 might be a fine source. But if you are reading a newspaper account of a new technique in genetic engineering, you should search for a more authoritative article on the same topic in a journal such as *Science* or a magazine like *Scientific American* (often the newspaper will mention its source of information within the article).

All this does not mean that you may never use newspapers or popular magazines as sources. Some magazines such as *Scientific American, Natural History, American Heritage,* and *The New Yorker* are less concerned with timeliness and brevity than with accuracy, and therefore they can require their authors to be as careful and precise as any scholar publishing in a journal. Even such magazines as *Time* and *Newsweek* often devote several pages to a single topic, normally a current issue or a notable person. These essays usually quote or paraphrase authoritative sources; in effect, these articles are informal research papers—informal because they lack footnotes and bibliographies—and are therefore usually acceptable sources for undergraduate research papers. In addition, these special reports are often written in clear, highly readable prose—a quality not always found in scholarly and professional journals.

As a general rule, however, you should not rely heavily on articles from newspapers and popular magazines as sources for your paper. Rather, use them to find clues to the information and ideas you will need, and follow up those clues by looking for more reliable sources of the same information.

Review Questions

1. What is a working bibliography? How does it differ from a final bibliography?
2. Write out the information for the following sources as you would on a bibliography card:

   - a 1952 book published in New York by Harcourt, Brace, & World called A History of Western Philosophy and written by W. T. Jones.
   - an article about the Japanese economy called How Japan Does It, written by Christopher Byron, published in Time magazine on March 30, 1981, and running from page 54 through page 60.
   - an article in The Sixteenth Century Journal by N. M. Sutherland called Catherine de Medici: The Legend of the Wicked Italian Queen, running from page 45 through page 56 and published in volume 9 in 1978.

3. Briefly outline the different but related processes of skimming a book and skimming a periodical article. What is the purpose of both types of skimming?
4. Explain how you can decide whether a potential source is likely to be useful to you. Mention several specific criteria.

Exercises

1. If you are presently working on a research project and have developed a topic and hypothesis, follow the suggestions in this chapter to put together a working bibliography and evaluate the potential sources by skimming them.
2. If you are not yet working on a research project, choose one of the topics and its accompanying hypothesis from the two examples on page 19. Assemble a working bibliography of about twelve potential sources, following the guidelines in this chapter. After evaluating the sources for their relevance to the chosen topic, skim them to see if they tend to support the hypothesis. Revise the hypothesis if it seems inaccurate.
3. In a popular magazine of your choice, read an article about a topic of current interest, such as *new energy sources, genetic engineering, political problems in Central America,* or *space probes of distant*

planets. Then, using an appropriate periodical index, find an article on the same topic in a professional journal, and read it. Write a paragraph or two contrasting the approaches used by the authors of the two articles.

4. Choose a nationally controversial topic, such as *the neutron bomb, medicaid payments for abortion, free agency in baseball, nuclear power plants, affirmative action programs,* or any important issue facing your area of the country. Find two articles in different periodicals (newspapers included) that take opposite sides on the issue. Write a one- to two-page paper summarizing their opposing views in some detail.

5

Reading the Sources and Taking Notes

When you begin reading your sources closely and taking notes, do not become so engrossed with recording information that you lose sight of your primary purpose and waste a good deal of time. Instead, look ahead to the research paper you intend to write, and, as always, keep your topic and hypothesis in mind as you are reading and taking notes. The information, ideas, and opinions you record should be those that you use when you write the paper.

Taking good notes is not a matter of simply copying down information, like taking names and numbers from a telephone directory. How useful your notes will be depends partly on the information you record and partly on the format in which you record it.

Practical Aspects of Note-taking

When you take notes from your sources, you do not know just how you will finally use each piece of information that you record. One thing, however, is certain: in your paper you will surely present your materials in a different order from that in which you happened to note them while you were reading. Since you do not yet know what sequence will be best, your notes should be recorded in a way that makes it easy for you to rearrange them and try out different sequences until you find the best one for your paper. But this is not possible if you have crammed your notes into a notebook, writing them on both sides of each page. There are two ways to solve this problem. Each has its advantages.

Preferred Method. Use four- by six-inch note cards and record just one idea, or a small group of closely related facts, on each card. Write notes on only one side of each card leaving the back free for bibliographic information. The main advantage of note cards is that after you have finished taking notes, you can spread the cards out on a table and rearrange them until you discover a satisfactory order. Another advantage is that the limited writing space available on a card will encourage you to avoid taking longer notes than you need.

Alternate Method. If you still feel more comfortable using a notebook, perhaps because you are worried that a card is easier to lose than a page in a notebook, write on just one side of each page and leave a fair amount of space between notes. This will allow you to cut each page into separate notes when you are ready to organize your paper.

Whatever method you use, be a big spender. Do not try to squeeze as many notes as possible into the space available. The satisfaction gained from being thrifty cannot compensate for the frustration of trying to untangle a tightly bunched, random assortment of facts and ideas.

ENTERING INFORMATION ON THE CARDS

When you are thinking about how to arrange information on an individual card, you need to anticipate two later steps in the research process. First, you will want to arrange the information according to *subtopics* when you construct an outline for your paper. Second, you must identify the precise source for each note, using all the bibliographical information plus the exact page or pages on which the information appeared. Here are some guidelines.

1. At the top of each card, note in pencil a possible subtopic—one which connects the information in that note to other information you expect to find. For example, the Jefferson Davis topic might be broken down into these subtopics: military strategy, conflicts with other leaders, poor health, cabinet choices, belief in Southern cause, and so on.

2. On the back of each card, identify the author and title of the source and the page or pages from which the information was taken.

These guidelines can be modified for use with a notebook.

1. Indicate the possible subtopic in the left margin next to the note.
2. Above each note, identify the author and title of the source and the page or pages from which the information was taken. To avoid confusion, draw a line below each note—even in a series of notes from a single source.

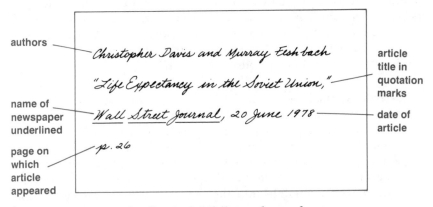

Figure 5–1. A three-by five-inch bibliography card

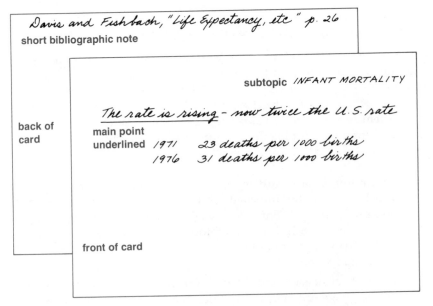

Figure 5–2. Front and back of a four-by six-inch note card

INFANT MORTALITY

Possible causes for recent rate increase

   1. More young mothers (15-19 yrs. old);
     more illegitimate births

   2. Many women don't use available
     health facilities and don't take
     good care of themselves when
     pregnant; many don't take
     children to doctors in time.

   3. (continued)

note is
continued
on following
card

(continued)   *INFANT MORTALITY*

(*Possible causes for rate increases*)

   3. Many women work and must return
     to jobs 2 mos. after delivery. The
     babies often go to day-care centers
     where they contract diseases
     (flu and pneumonia)

   4. NOT the result of Soviet health-
     care system, which is improving.

Figure 5–3. A series of notes continued on a second card

The Fine Art of Note-taking

As we have said, effective note-taking consists of more than copying relevant passages out of your sources. In fact, the more direct copying you do, the less useful your notes are likely to be. Here is why.

Note-taking for a research paper has three fundamental objectives:

- to record the general ideas that will form the backbone of your research paper,

- to record specific pieces of information that support the general ideas, and
- to preserve the exact wording of some statements in your sources that you may want to quote in the paper.

Many students waste time copying down long passages, even whole pages, word for word, because they believe wrongly that research papers must contain a large number of quotations. This is just not so. In fact, the opposite is true. For most research assignments, you should restrict the use of quotation to at most 20 percent of the paper. (Of course, this limit does not apply to those topics for which you must quote from literary works as well as from your sources.) For some topics, especially in the natural sciences, excellent papers can be produced without using any quotations at all.

One important reason for limiting the amount of quotation is that by stating most of the ideas and information in the paper in your own words, you show your readers that you understand what you are talking about. Another reason is that producing a coherent paper from a collection of quotations is almost impossible. Even though it might seem easier to quote than to paraphrase and summarize, the resulting "paper" would amount to a confusing, tenuously related set of statements. Actually, it is easier to express most of the ideas and information in your own words than to wrestle with a mass of quotations.

Paraphrasing

To paraphrase is to express another person's idea in your own words. The value of paraphrasing goes far beyond meeting the requirement that you find your own way of saying what you have found in your sources. For one thing, a good paraphrase usually takes fewer words than the original to convey the essential meaning. Even more important is the increased understanding that comes from trying to paraphrase what you are reading. Psychological experiments have shown that putting a difficult idea into your own words makes a stronger impression on your memory than merely copying the idea word for word. In fact, if you have trouble restating an idea, you probably do not thoroughly understand it. In general, therefore, paraphrase any ideas that go into your notes unless there is a good reason for quoting the exact words in the source. (Several common situations that call for quotation are discussed on pages 79–81.)

The following examples reveal two benefits to be gained from paraphrasing: brevity and clarity.

original   Will reputable scientists ever accept the claim that ex-
                        trasensory perception and other paranormal powers
                        really exist? It appears that many of them have.

paraphrase   Many scientists today believe in the reality
                        of ESP and other paranormal powers.

The idea of "reputable" is not needed in your note; you know that
you are looking only for real scientists—not those who simply call
themselves scientists, as do some who work with ESP.

original   Olfactory receptors for communication between differ-
                        ent creatures are crucial for establishment of symbiotic
                        relations.

paraphrases   The sense of smell is essential to cooperation
                        among different animal species.

                        Cooperation between different animal species
                        is made possible by their sense of smell.

Summarizing

A summary greatly reduces the length of what you have read, which
might be anything from a long paragraph to an entire magazine article.
Writing effective summaries requires good judgment, for you must
decide what can be left out of your notes without losing or distorting
the basic idea.

If you are working on a single paragraph, you may find that it contains a clearly stated topic sentence that is aptly supported by several
details. In that case, you can simply paraphrase the main idea and then
decide whether you need to note briefly any of the details, either for
use in your paper or to reinforce your understanding of the main idea.
In the following example, the main idea is stated in the first sentence,
as is the case in much professional writing.

original   Zoologists define *species* as a category of animals whose
                        members are capable of mating and producing offspring
                        which are also able to reproduce. Thus, dogs constitute
                        a species because even males and females of the most
                        dissimilar breeds can produce mongrels that can, in
                        turn, reproduce. However, the mating of a horse and
                        a donkey, though the two are more similar in appear-
                        ance than, let us say, a poodle and a boxer, yields a

mule, which is always sterile. Thus, they are placed in separate species. A lion and a tiger, though of different species, can produce a "liger" or a "tiglon," which in very rare cases may be fertile. This exception betrays a slight weakness in our definition of the term *species*.

summary
note card

Species

Definition of species — mating

Two animals are said to belong to the same species if they can produce fertile offspring.

*Ex: poodle + boxer but not
horse + donkey (mule is sterile)*

Whether or not you should include details in your note depends on your purpose. If your note is intended only to make sure you remember the definition of *species,* you probably do not need the parenthetical examples. If you intend to develop the concept of *species* in your paper, you may need them. The example of the "liger" and the "tiglon" would be needed only if you planned to discuss the fact that a scientific term can be less precise than most of us believe.

Often your summary of a paragraph will consist of a general idea that you have derived from several details in the paragraph which directly relate to your hypothesis. Assume when reading the next example that you are gathering information related to the hypothesis, "Most scientists now believe that life probably exists on planets circling other stars in the universe."

original

The sun is accompanied on its journey through space by a retinue of nine planets, thirty-two natural satellites revolving around the planets, hundreds of comets and thousands of asteroids. Do other stars have similar arrays of companions? At present there is no direct way of telling, because if such a collection of bodies were associated with a nearby star, the most powerful telescopes on the earth could not detect them. The feeble light reflected from the companions would be lost in the brilliant glare of the central star.

Helmut A. Abt, "The Companions of Sunlike Stars"
Sci. Amer., April 1977

LIFE-SUPPORTING PLANETS

Do systems like our solar system exist?

Other stars may have planets, but
the strongest telescopes can't pick
them out because of the brightness
of the stars.

**summary
note card**

The background information at the beginning of the original paragraph has been left out of the summary because you do not need it to understand the main idea—that even if other stars have planets on which life might exist, these planets cannot be seen by our telescopes. This example illustrates another way to keep your notes brief. If some of the background information had been new to you, you might have been tempted to add it to your notes, just because it was unfamiliar. Doing so would not have helped you when you came to write your paper. Use your hypothesis to guide you in deciding whether such information is truly relevant to your purposes.

Quoting

Once you accept the principle that you should paraphrase or summarize most of the ideas that go into your notes, you will be better able to judge when quotation can be both appropriate and effective. There are four common reasons for quoting from your sources—_conciseness, accuracy, memorable language,_ and _authority._

Sometimes your best efforts at paraphrasing will produce a version that is either longer and clumsier than the original or else somewhat inaccurate. In either case, you should quote all or part of the original statement. On other occasions, a source may express an idea so brilliantly that you want to preserve its beauty and power. Finally, you may want to support an idea or one of your conclusions by quoting a key statement or two from an established authority on the subject. None of these reasons for quoting is, however, an excuse for avoiding the effort necessary to create a successful paraphrase. You must learn to recognize those special times when these reasons are likely to be valid.

Examples of four situations in which direct quotation is desirable are presented below, along with some further advice on when to quote rather than paraphrase or summarize. The examples consist of note cards and of excerpts from research papers that show how the quotations were eventually put to use.

Conciseness: *You find that you cannot paraphrase an idea without using many more words than the source.*

A common instance of this occurs when you decide to introduce a specialized term into your paper. You think it should be defined, but your attempts to paraphrase a definition are all long and awkward. In that case, you should quote part or most of the definition from the source.

excerpt from paper

Noam Chomsky has been called a reductionist-- someone who believes that "all complex phenomena are ultimately explained and understood by analyzing them into increasingly simpler and supposedly more elementary components."[1] Professor Chomsky, however, does not accept this label.

. . . . .

[1] N. H. Pronko, <u>Panorama of Psychology</u> (Belmont, Calif.: Wadsworth, 1969), p. 497.

The footnote refers to the source of the definition, a textbook that the student used solely for the definition and not for any information related to Professor Chomsky. That textbook, however, must be included in the bibliography, or list of references, for the research paper, and the student therefore made out a bibliography card for the source and a note card for the quote.

Accuracy: *You find that you cannot paraphrase an idea without distorting the author's meaning.*

If, for example, a writer said that "virtually all women have experienced fantasies in which they were born as men," any paraphrase is likely to be more or less inaccurate.

possible paraphrases: Most women wish they were men.

The first is grossly
distorted; the second   The majority of women have dreamed that they
is closer but not   were men.
entirely accurate; the
third is accurate but
longer than the   Almost every woman has had a dream or a
original.   daydream in which she has been born a male.

In such cases, you would do much better to quote the source and let your readers draw their own conclusions and compare them with the interpretations that you advance in your paper.

Along the same lines, you may come across a remark which is so startling that your readers might not believe that a paraphrase is entirely accurate. For instance, an outstanding biologist, J. B. S. Haldane, described Albert Einstein as "the greatest Jew since Jesus." Such a striking comment surely deserves to be quoted rather than paraphrased.

Memorable Language: *You believe that the words chosen by your source are so vivid or powerful that they lend a meaning that cannot be captured in a paraphrase.*

Restrain yourself in this matter; beware of quoting someone merely because he or she "says it so much better than I could." An example of brilliant language that cries out for quotation comes from a speech by Winston Churchill which refers to the behavior of Soviet Russia as "a riddle wrapped in a mystery inside an enigma."

In the same vein, you should feel free to quote famous remarks even if the word choice is neither brilliant nor difficult to paraphrase. An example would be President Truman's advice for timid politicians: "If you can't stand the heat, get out of the kitchen."

Authority: *You want to support a conclusion you have reached in your research by quoting the words of an expert on the subject.*

The authors of most of your sources are experts on their subjects, at least in the sense that their ideas have been thought authoritative enough to publish. This guideline, then, should be used selectively. In general, even experts should be quoted only when their words are more concise, accurate, or memorable than any paraphrase or summary you can make. When you are trying to prove a point, do not rely entirely upon expert opinion, whether quoted or paraphrased. Be sure that your conclusion is supported by other evidence—facts and reasoning.

QUOTING IN CONTEXT

Since you are always quoting just a small part of any source, you must take great care to see that everything *which you did not quote* agrees with the idea which you did quote. This principle applies to paraphrasing as well, of course. The next example shows how someone could read a passage hastily and then produce a serious misrepresentation of its author's meaning.

student's source

It is currently very fashionable among popular social critics to blame television for the recent widespread increase in juvenile crime statistics. The argument usually pursues this line of reasoning. Many parents today neglect their children by allowing them complete freedom in watching TV. The shows these children choose to watch often present violence in an attractive form, and some have even gone so far as to depict clever ways of committing crimes. Many of these children later re-enact the violent acts they have witnessed on TV in order to recapture the thrills.

I contend, however, that this widely accepted explanation of a serious social problem is too simplistic. . . .

If someone used that passage to produce the following quotation he or she would grossly distort the writer's meaning.

quotation out of context

Sociologist Jane Doe joins those persons who denounce violence on TV as the primary cause of the sharp increase in the number of crimes committed by young people: "Many . . . children later re-enact the violent acts they have witnessed on TV in order to recapture the thrills." . . .

BLENDING QUOTATION WITH PARAPHRASE

The most effective way to avoid quoting too many words from a particular passage is to combine quotation with paraphrase. A good guideline to follow when you are quoting is to quote only as much of a passage as is necessary to fulfill your specific purpose.

Were you to read the full speech in which Churchill made his famous remark about Russia, you would see the advantage of choosing carefully what to quote. Churchill's speech was an attempt to alleviate Britain's fears that Russia might not enter the war against Nazi Germany. Part of that speech is presented here, along with a note card showing how quotation can be blended with paraphrase or summary.

original speech — I cannot forecast to you the action of Russia. It is a riddle wrapped in a mystery inside an enigma; but perhaps there is a key. That key is Russian national interest. It cannot be in accordance with the interest or safety of Russia that Germany should plant itself upon the shores of the Black Sea, or that it should overrun the Balkan states and subjugate the Slavonic peoples of Southeastern Europe. That would be contrary to the historic life interests of Russia.

Vital Speeches of the Day, 1 Oct. 1939

C. on Russian foreign policy

(late 1939)

The English were wondering whether R. would go to war against Nazi Germany. C. described R's policy as "a riddle wrapped in a mystery inside an enigma." He added that the key to the riddle was "Russian national interest" and this led him to predict that R. wod. enter the war.

summary
note card

ENTERING QUOTATIONS ON NOTECARDS

When writing a note, you must indicate with absolute accuracy which words, if any, come directly from the source. Otherwise you may accidentally use a published author's words as your own, and that is plagiarism. Naturally, you mark off quotations with quotation marks, but there's more to it than that. Several problems can occur when you are reviewing your notes and preparing to write the paper. Thinking about these problems in advance can lead you to adopt procedures to prevent any possible confusion.

Since quotation marks are small they can be overlooked when you are transferring information from your notes to your paper. To avoid missing a quotation mark or two, use very heavy strokes or even the marks « and ». This will insure against your confusing quoted material with a paraphrase.

If your note summarizes several pages of a source, and includes a quotation, you must record the page number where the quotation appeared:

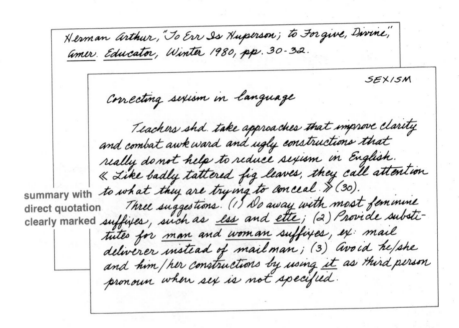

Herman Arthur, "To Err Is Huperson; to Forgive, Divine," *Amer. Educator*, Winter 1980, pp. 30-32.

SEXISM

Correcting sexism in language

Teachers shd. take approaches that improve clarity and combat awkward and ugly constructions that really do not help to reduce sexism in English. « Like badly tattered fig leaves, they call attention to what they are trying to conceal » (30).

Three suggestions. (1) Do away with most feminine suffixes, such as *ess* and *ette*; (2) Provide substitutes for *man* and *woman* suffixes, ex: mail deliverer instead of mailman; (3) Avoid he/she and him/her constructions by using *it* as third person pronoun when sex is not specified.

summary with direct quotation clearly marked

In your effort to limit the length of quoted material, you will often find it possible to leave some words out of the middle of a quotation because they are not relevant to your purpose. The question is how to indicate this omission, which a reader is entitled to know about if you use the quote in your paper. The answer is to use an *ellipsis*, which consists of three spaced dots substituted for the omitted passage. The example shows a passage from a research paper in which a quotation was shortened by ellipsis. The passage also demonstrates a blend of direct quotation and paraphrase.

student's source

Literature is slow to register its own historical moment. Only in the past few years has a literature announcing the end of the 1960s emerged. It isn't generally a literature *about* that decade; apart from the novels of Marge Piercy and a few scenes in Mary Gordon's *The Company of Women,* there isn't much description of the tableaux that represent the sixties: rock concerts, riots, campus demonstrations. Purposeful collective acts have given way to private anomie. The predominant mood in the novels and stories of Jayne Anne Phillips, Richard Ford, Mary Robison, Ann Beattie, and Raymond Carver—to mention five younger writers who have begun to command an audience—is indifference, depression, even criminality. Such is fiction's bleak requiem for that turbulent era.

**excerpt from
student's paper**

The critic James Atlas believes that "a literature announcing the end of the 1960s" has only come into being as we move into the 1980s, and it does not present those public events that marked "that turbulent era," such as student demonstrations against the war, riots in the inner cities, and rock concerts. "Purposeful collective acts have given way to private anomie. The predominant mood . . . is indifference, depression, even criminality."[8]

. . . . .

[8]James Atlas, "Less is Less," <u>Atlantic Monthly</u>, June 1981, p. 96.

One last problem concerns a source that may itself contain a quotation that you choose to note. The possible danger here is that you might not remember whether the quoted words in your notes are those of the source's author or those of the person the source was quoting. Use standard quotation marks (" and ") or single guillemets (‹ and ›), written heavily, to mark off the quotation within the source.

student's source

Of all the Concord circle Emerson was perhaps the most widely read in science. He was familiar with Sir Charles Lyell's work in geology and was well aware that Christian chronology had become a mere "kitchen clock" compared with the vast time depths the earth sciences were beginning to reveal. "What terrible questions we are learning to ask," brooded the man sometimes accused of walking with his head in the clouds. He saw us as already divesting ourselves of the theism of our fathers.

Loren Eiseley, "Man Against the Universe." *The Star Thrower* (New York: Harcourt Brace Jovanovich, 1978) p.212

RWE / Science / Faith

Religion vs. Science

Emerson knew a good deal about current scientific advances, e.g. Sir Charles Lyell's geological theories. E. believed that ≪ Christian chronology had become a mere "kitchen clock" compared with the vast time depths the earth sciences were beginning to reveal. "what terrible questions we are learning to ask," ≫ said E., who realized Americans were moving away from the ≪ theism of our fathers. ≫

summary
card with
quotations

An Extended Example of Effective Note-taking

To illustrate the process of note-taking, an article that served as a source for a paper on ESP follows. Accompanying the article is a full set of note cards derived from it. First, notice how the student's hypothesis limits the amount of information that has to be recorded. Also note the student's reasoning for deciding what to quote, paraphrase, or summarize.

Student's hypothesis: "Modern scientific techniques are being used to investigate ESP, and the results have convinced some leading scientists that parapsychology is a valid field of study."

Arguing the Existence of ESP

By MALCOLM W. BROWNE

Browne's thesis takes the form of a question and its answer. The research that went into this article may have grown out of that question.

A more detailed statement of the thesis follows. No note is needed. The idea as presented here is too vague for use in a paper. Further mention of this work later in the article is more specific.

No note should be recorded. This information is interesting, but it is not directly related to the student's hypothesis.

WILL reputable scientists ever accept the claim that extrasensory perception and other "paranormal powers" really exist?

It appears that many of them already have.

Not only do some of the world's most honored scientists believe in parapsychology, but a newly published survey suggests that a majority of American scientists accept at least the possibility that extrasensory perception really exists.

A rash of new parapsychology experiments drawing ideas from the physics of atomic particles has rekindled an old controversy over whether parapsychology is a legitimate science or merely a pseudoscience created by charlatans to snare the naïve.

Results Are Reported

Some experimenters claim that the natural process of radioactive decay can be influenced by mental concentration, and that results of their latest work demonstrate the contention. Other experiments purport to show that mind power alone can change the temperature of supersensitive thermometers and the separation between objects. Some respected scientists have turned to meditation as a means of seeking truth.

Various laboratories have sought to either confirm or debunk the legitimacy of parapsychology since the controversial 1930's experiments by Dr. Joseph Banks Rhine of Duke University. Dr.

note
card 1

> poll of scientists re: ESP
>
> <u>poll</u> conducted by Dr. Mahlon Wagner, psychologist
> State Univ. of N.Y., Oswego
>
> published in <u>Zetetic</u> <u>Scholar</u>, journal that
> often attacks claims of ESP.
>
> Wagner: « "I used to be a total skeptic...
> but I've become a little more accepting
> because there are good, honest scholars
> in the field." »
>   (of parapsychology)
>   (continued)

note
card 2

> poll of scientists   re: ESP
>
> <u>poll sent to 2,100 professors</u> across country
>   1,188 answered
>
> of the « natural scientists » who answered—
>
>   9% « accepted extrasensory perception as
>   an "established fact" »
>   45% « described ESP as a "likely
>   possibility." »

Rhine had his subjects try to use supposed paranormal powers to "see" the designs on special cards concealed from them.

His results proved, he contended, that extrasensory perception permits subjects to pick the right cards significantly more often than chance alone would allow.

Conclusions Challenged

Other scientists challenged this conclusion, noting that Dr. Rhine and other parapsychologists routinely reject data from subjects who are not performing well. If all the data from extrasensory perception tests were preserved and reckoned into the statistics, critics say, the statistics would show a result no better than pure chance.

The parapsychologists have argued that paranormal abilities cannot be turned on or off like laboratory apparatus, and that it is fair to discard results from subjects who are not "on."

The dispute over this key question has never been resolved, and belief in parapsychology, like religion, remains a matter of faith. Despite that, belief by scientists in psychic phenomena seems to be far more widespread than many had suspected.

Dr. Mahlon Wagner, a psychologist at the Oswego campus of the State University of New York, recently published in the journal Zetetic Scholar the results of a poll he conducted. The journal, whose name is derived from the Greek word for skeptic, publishes scholarly papers, most of which attack claims of paranormal phenomena.

Dr. Wagner sent questionnaires to 2,100 professors at colleges and universities throughout the country, and received 1,188 responses. Of the natural scientists who responded, he said, 9 percent said they accepted extrasensory perception as an "established fact," and 45 percent described ESP as "a likely possibility."

How does Dr. Wagner himself feel about his results?

No note is needed. The sentence merely restates the article's thesis.

See note cards 1 and 2.

note
card 3

Scientists researching in parapsych.

1. Dr. Robert G. Jahn, dean of engineering
   and applied science at Princeton
   — can mental powers change a thermometer
   reading or the distance between objects?

2. Dr. Peter F. Phillips, physicist, Washington
   Univ. (St. Louis)
   received grant of $500,000 for «psychic
   research» from McDonnell Douglas
   Corp. foundation.

note
card 4

recognition of parasych. by
scientific world

American Physical Society

1979 annual meeting held special session
on parapsychology, though most
attending were skeptical.

Dr. Helmut Schmidt described his
experiments with ESP.

see Schmidt cards

note
card 5

Radioactive decay experiments
SCHMIDT

S. built machine in which radioactivity
randomly turns on lights, one at a
time. Lights are arranged in a circle.

«Subjects are asked to try to influence
the direction in which the lights
come on.»
Results —
«Significant correlation between subjects'
mental efforts and the observed
results.»

See note card 3.

No note is needed. The information is interesting but not relevant to the student's hypothesis.

See note card 4.

See note card 5.

"I used to be a total skeptic," he said, speaking of parapsychology, "but I've become a little more accepting because there are good, honest scholars in the field."

Research in parapsychology has been spurred by a number of recent financial grants.

Backed by private donors, Dr. Robert G. Jahn, dean of engineering and applied science at Princeton University, has undertaken a psychic research program based on some experiments that suggested mind power might change a thermometer reading or the distance between two objects.

Another physicist, Dr. Peter F. Phillips of Washington University in St. Louis, was awarded a $500,000 grant several months ago for psychic research. The grant, one of the largest ever made for psychic research, was from a foundation established by the McDonnell Douglas Corporation.

There have been hints that American intelligence organizations have experimented with ESP, and Soviet security officials interrogated and expelled an American news correspondent for allegedly receiving a secret research report on parapsychology.

At the annual meeting of the prestigious American Physical Society last year, a special session on parapsychology was held for the first time, and although most of those attending were deeply skeptical, some 500 scientists listened attentively to such parapsychologists as Helmut Schmidt of the Mind Science Foundation of San Antonio, Tex., an institution maintained by grants from William Thomas Slick Jr., a Texas oil magnate.

Dr. Schmidt, a physicist by training, uses devices called random-number generators in his experiments. These machines are actuated by the random quantum-mechanical process of radioactive decay, producing a continuous series of numbers.

Describing his experiments in an interview, Dr. Schmidt said one of his machines has a ring of lights arranged

Radioactive decay experiments
SCHMIDT

Variation on experiment

Machine lit lights <u>before</u> the people were
asked to use their ES power, but people
weren't told about it.

Results —
Same as on first test. Schmidt says this
seems to show that ES power can work
《" backward in time, and that is an outrageous
idea from a conventional standpoint." 》 May be
due to some 《 quantum effects 》 scientists don't
understand.

radioactive decay experiments
SCHMIDT

Criticism of Schmidt's conclusions

Paul Horowitz, physicist, Chairman of the
Amer. Physical Soc. parapsych. session —

Schmidt 《 probably wrong 》 but
H. believes that scientists should continue to investigate parapsych.

Scientists attack ESP

John A. Wheeler, physicist working on black hole theory

parapsych is a 《" pretentious pseudoscience" 》
when its experiments are examined by
rigorous scientific methods. They 《 prove
nothing. 》

Wheeler wd. like Parapsych. Assn. to lose status
as Amer. Assn. for the Advancement of
Science affiliate.

like a clock dial, and the radioactive process randomly illuminates one of these lights at a time. Subjects are asked to try to influence the direction in which the lights come on. The results, he asserted, demonstrated a significant correlation between his subjects' mental efforts and the observed results.

See note card 6.

In another type of experiment, Dr. Schmidt said he gave subjects the same instructions, but unknown to them, the machine had already produced its random series of numbers the previous day. Electronic recordings had been made of the numbers and stored in a safe without being examined. Copies made from them were then played for the subjects, who believed they were watching the machine in action rather than a mere recording.

Again, Dr. Schmidt said, there was correlation between their mental efforts and the results, even though the results had been obtained beforehand. "The implication seems to be that the effect can work backward in time," he said, "and that is an outrageous idea from a conventional standpoint. But it may be that some quantum effects not yet understood could account for just such an outcome."

See note card 7.

The chairman of the parapsychology session, Paul Horowitz of Cambridge, Mass., a physicist, asserted that Dr. Schmidt was "probably wrong." "But it's important that the investigation of parapsychology be kept within the structure of science where it can be examined critically," he said.

See note card 8.

Some scientists are outraged by such thinking.

Among them is John A. Wheeler, an American physicist specializing in the theory of gravitational collapse and "black holes."

Contending that parapsychology is a "pretentious pseudoscience," he has sought for the past year to have the Parapsychological Association based in Alexandria, Va., deprived of its status as an affiliate of the American Association for the Advancement of Science.

Scientists attack ESP

John G. Taylor, mathematician at King's Coll., London, once believed but now does not. 1975 book, <u>Superminds</u>, supported parapsych.

T. had been convinced that Uri Geller, Israeli psychic, could bend spoons and move objects solely by mental power.

After Geller's tricks were exposed, Dr. Taylor wrote two papers recanting his earlier position.

Scientists support ESP

Sir William Crookes
Wolfgang Pauli

《 giants of physics 》

Still believe in spite of numerous exposures of psychics like Uri Geller.

Scientists support ESP
JOSEPHSON
Brian Josephson — Nobel prize in physics, 1973
Cambridge Univ.

《 has increasingly turned toward parapsych. during the past 10 years in his research. 》

is 《 "99% convinced" 》 that 《 "remote viewing" 》 and 《 metal bending 》 are real.

See note card 9.

See note cards 10 and 11.

No note is needed since scientists are expected to think rigorously.

Dr. Wheeler and other scientific critics of parapsychology maintain that when results from psychic experiments are scrutinized according to accepted scientific and statistical tests they turn out to prove nothing.

Despite such objections, scientists are as often duped by charlatans and hoaxsters as are nonscientists, skeptics assert.

A case in point, they say, is that of John G. Taylor, a distinguished mathematician at King's College, London, who wrote a popular book in 1975 called "Superminds." The book, which was essentially a testimonial for parapsychology, recounted how Dr. Taylor had become convinced by the demonstrations of a self-styled psychic from Israel named Uri Geller. Mr. Geller claimed to be able to bend spoons, transport objects through the air and perform many other tricks by mental power alone.

Later, when Mr. Geller's feats were revealed as mere tricks of stagecraft, Dr. Taylor published two papers in the scientific journal Nature, recanting his earlier endorsement.

But many similar cases over the years have failed to shake the convictions of a number of distinguished scientists, including two giants of physics, Sir William Crookes and Wolfgang Pauli.

Dr. Brian Josephson, a 40-year-old British scientist who was awarded the Nobel physics prize in 1973, has increasingly turned toward parapsychology during the past 10 years in his research at Cavendish Laboratory, Cambridge University, England. (The latter institution awarded its first doctorate in parapsychology last year.)

In a telephone interview, Dr. Josephson said he was "99 percent convinced" of the reality of the paranormal effects, notably "remote viewing" and mental metal bending.

Dr. Josephson's mastery of quantum mechanics and other hard physical principles led him to discovery of the Josephson effect, by which electrical

Scientists support ESP
JOSEPHSON

《 "to some extent ... parapsych. lies within
the bounds of physical law." 》
《 but physical law itself may have to be redefined ... It may be that some effects in
parapsych. are ordered - state effects
of a kind not yet encompassed by
physical theory." 》

In this sense, the study of parapsych. is
similar to the study of intelligence
and consciousness.

conductivity in an ultra-cold environment can be switched on or off with a magnetic field. Super computers of the coming decade are expected to be based on it. Is the rigorous technique of thought that discovered the Josephson effect compatible with parapsychology?

See note card 12.

"You ask whether parapsychology lies within the bounds of physical law," Dr. Josephson said. "My feeling is that to some extent it does, but physical law itself may have to be redefined in terms of some new principles. It may be that some effects in parapsychology are ordered-state effects of a kind not yet encompassed by physical theory.

"My interest is not only in parapsychology but in the nature of intelligence and consciousness. These are also ordered processes which are not yet understood," he said. "It may be that an understanding of intelligence and consciousness lies outside the paradigm of physics. It may be that more can be learned about the nature of reality through meditative processes."

But he did not expect the results of such work to be universally persuasive.

"It is clear," he said, "that you can never satisfy a skeptic except by enrolling him directly in an experiment, and you can't do that with every skeptic."

The Problem of Plagiarism

Plagiarism is one of the worst offenses a writer can commit, comparable with distorting or inventing evidence. It is a kind of theft: one writer steals the ideas or even the actual words of another writer without giving credit where it is due. Plagiarism is so serious that if you publish plagiarized work, you can be sued. The author of a famous book recently ended up paying another writer many thousands of dollars because the book contained passages which resembled the other writer's earlier work almost word for word. Plagiarism in academic writing can also be severely punished. For this reason you should take great care to use footnotes to let your readers know whenever you use ideas or information that came from one of your sources.

Earlier, we mentioned that it is possible to plagiarize by accident. In using an idea from a source, you might carelessly fail to insert a footnote, and so it would appear that you were trying to claim that an idea was your own or that you had discovered a piece of information through your own efforts. If you commit such an oversight, it is easy enough to correct. Simply reread your paper, with your note cards and bibliography cards at hand, and check each significant concept or fact against your notes to see where it came from and whether you have given proper credit. Where necessary, add any source citations you omitted.

The problem of plagiarizing another author's language may not be so easy to deal with. So many of your notes will consist of paraphrases and summaries that you might accidentally treat one of your direct quotations as though it, too, had been written in your own words. If in taking notes you followed our suggestion and marked off the quotations with large quotation marks, or « and », then you can easily check your paper against your notes to be sure all quotations are identified as such. If the markings on your note cards are not clear, however, you must go back to the actual sources to determine which words in your notes are quotations and which are your own.

The problem of plagiarizing language, however, usually goes beyond copying full sentences or even paragraphs from a source without using quotation marks and footnotes. Some students find themselves suspected of plagiarism because the wording of their paraphrases is so close to that of the original passages that they are practically quoting. Only a few words are changed, and the sentence patterns are virtually identical to those in the sources. Here is an example.

This passage comes from a description of George Washington's plan for saving his army from the British, who had trapped him into defending a fortress on the shore of Long Island. The only means of escape required moving the men in small boats.

original passage | The other necessity, and this seemed the impossible one, was for Washington to find some way to get his army away without tremendous loss. The problem was that, when part of the force was on water, the rest, unable adequately to defend the fortifications, would become easy prey for the enemy. Unless he could somehow slip secretly away, Washington would have to sacrifice half his army.

a case of laziness or
deliberate
plagiarism?

The other need, which seemed to be impossible,
was for Washington to discover some means of
getting the army away without enormous losses.
His problem was that, when some of the
soldiers were on the water, the others would
be unable to defend their land position
adequately and could be easily defeated by the
British. Unless Washington could manage to
slip away in secret, he would lose half his
forces.[1]

. . . . .

[1] James T. Flexner, The Young Hamilton
(Boston: Little, Brown, 1978), p.110.

Perhaps the only crime here is laziness, but the fact remains that this student relied very heavily upon the original sentence structure and only "translated" the passage by finding synonyms for a few words. Although the footnote tells the reader where the information came from, there is no indication that the wording is not entirely the student's own work. This example of plagiarism may not have been intentional. The student may have thought that since the two versions are not exactly the same, no plagiarism occurred. But his version sounds too much like the original. In order to repair the damage, he would have to rewrite the entire paragraph, changing the sentence structure and finding different word choices.

acceptable
paraphrase

Washington's brilliance as a field commander
is shown by his plan for the army to escape by
water before the British knew what was
happening. Obviously, the soldiers could not
simply board boats and sail away, because, if
the British attacked in the middle of the
operation, most of the troops would be in no
position to defend themselves.[1]

. . . . .

[1] James T. Flexner, The Young Hamilton
(Boston: Little, Brown, 1978), p. 110.

This paraphrase is distinctly different from the source, as it should be. Of course, a footnote is still essential—to credit the author as the source of the information.

It is not always easy to know how different from the original your paraphrase must be if you are to avoid plagiarism. A possible rule would be to enclose any words found in a source within quotation marks, but this could lead to absurdities in many common situations. For instance, how would you paraphrase the following sentence without using the italicized words?

original

The typical *Inuit igloo* offers superior insulation against *temperatures* that fall as low as *−50° F.*

There are no synonyms for many personal nouns, such as *Inuit,* just as there are no synonyms for most numbers (exceptions: *dozen* for *12; score* for *20; decade* for *ten years*). As for *igloo,* the substitution of *ice house* or *house made from blocks of hard-packed snow* would be either inaccurate or very clumsy, and *temperature* can only be replaced by a slightly different idea, such as *coldness* or *freezing weather.* If you put quotation marks around these words in your paraphrase, the result would look rather silly:

absurd use of
quotation marks

```
A well-made "Inuit igloo" can protect its
occupants even when "temperatures" outside
reach "-50° F."
```

Obviously, any rule must be more flexible than this. In general, then, you can safely repeat specific numbers (*−50° F., 21 percent, 5,280 feet, seven million people, $524.52*), special terms for which there is no simple synonym (*igloo, gross national product, income tax, influenza, touchdown, amphetamine*), and even very simple words that would require bizarre substitutions (*horse*—not *graminivorous quadruped, ocean, atmosphere, lung, father, high school, temperature*).

Remember, however, that sometimes even a single word taken from a source requires quotation marks if it is especially colorful or represents the writer's judgment. The following summary of an article quoted just three isolated words.

student summary of
article

```
In 1912, H. H. Goddard, director of research
at Vineland Institute for Feeble-minded Girls
and Boys in New Jersey, was commissioned by
the U.S. Public Health Service to survey
mental deficiency among immigrant populations
at Ellis Island. Goddard's study employed
"ridiculous" criteria which led to "absurd"
conclusions regarding the native intelligence
of Jews and other unpopular European
minorities. Goddard's work played a
significant role in the passage of the
```

Restriction Act of 1924, which, according to
Allan Chase, author of The Legacy of Malthus,
barred millions of Jews from entering the
United States and thereby escaping the Nazi
holocaust.[10]

. . . . .

[10] Stephen Jay Gould, "Science and Jewish
Immigration," Natural History, Dec. 1980, pp.
14–19.

As you can see, the problem concerns not only individual words but also the flow of thought and the presentation of ideas, which combine to give a piece of writing its style and originality.

In summary, the research paper is intended to measure, among other things, your ability to express ideas effectively. Although this challenge can be frustrating at times, you are expected to maintain a personal integrity that will prevent your surrendering to the temptation to borrow even "just a little bit here and there" from your sources.

Review Questions

1. How does a hypothesis help you to read sources and take good notes?

2. What kind of information *must* be recorded on every note card to avoid problems at later stages in the process? Where should this information be entered on a card?

3. Why do successful note-takers keep each note as brief as possible?

4. What is the difference between a summary and a paraphrase? How are they similar?

5. What are the advantages of paraphrasing and summarizing rather than copying passages from sources?

6. When paraphrasing, do you have to change every word that appeared in the original? Explain your answer.

7. Roughly what proportion of your notes is likely to consist of direct quotation from the sources? Why?

8. For what reasons might you quote rather than paraphrase a statement found in a source?

9. Why might plagiarism become a problem even for very honest writers of research papers?

Exercises

1. Take notes on this newspaper article, using the hypothesis and subtopics to judge the usefulness of the information you read. Remember not to crowd information onto your cards; you will probably need more than one card for each subtopic. Be sure to mark any quotations very clearly. In parentheses, next to each quote, indicate your reason for quoting (conciseness, accuracy, memorable language, authority).

Topic: *social action that deals with the problems of the elderly*

Hypothesis: "The problems that afflict people late in life have recently become a major national concern."

Suggested subtopics: 1. causes of senility; 2. diagnosing senility; 3. senility as a social problem

Senility Is Not Always What It Seems to Be

By LAWRENCE K. ALTMAN

The brain of a young adult contains about 12 billion neurons, the cells that send nerve impulses through the body's most complex organ, and each day, as part of the aging process, the brain shrinks from the death of 100,000 neurons. After decades of losing these irreplaceable cells in an uneven pattern through the brain, the mind of the older individual may wander and he may no longer be able to care for himself. In a word, he becomes senile.

Lapses of memory are common, and when an older person forgets an appointment or name, he is naturally inclined to ask, "Am I getting senile?" In most cases, the answer is in the negative because humans are fallible at all ages, and most older people are not senile.

Nevertheless, the problem of senility is becoming increasingly important. Sometimes, the problem comes to dramatic public attention as it did last week when a California Supreme Court justice was ordered to retire because of senility. But the cases of hundreds of thousands of other senile people who manage to carry out their jobs and daily household activities with varying degrees of success receive far less publicity despite the magnitude of the affliction.

Geriatric specialists estimate that 15 percent of people 65 to 75 years old and 25 percent of those 75 and older are senile, a total of about four million. The National Institutes of Health say that 60 percent of the 950,000 nursing home patients over the age of 65 are senile. No accurate statistics exist to know if a larger percentage of older people are getting senile or if there are more senile people because there are more older people. But some geriatricians express the belief that for unknown reasons senility is truly increasing.

Nor do doctors know the cause of senility. It appears to be more than just the loss of neurons, because many older people who have shrunken brains maintain keen minds, and some senile people do not have unusually small brains. And doctors do not know if senility is a disease or a natural aging condition that would affect everyone who lived long enough.

For unknown reasons, the loss of neurons occurs unevenly in the brain, seemingly affecting the frontal and temporal lobes (which among other things play key roles in verbalization and hearing) more than other areas of the organ.

Doctors who have studied senile changes have often found it difficult to pinpoint the exact nature of the anatomical brain changes and even more difficult to correlate such changes with the patient's symptoms.

Senility—the word is derived from the Latin word meaning old—is a condition generally characterized by memory loss, particularly for recent events, loss of ability to do simple arithmetic problems, and disorientation to time and place. It is a diagnosis doctors must make by impression, primarily by a bedside examination, because they have no specific diagnostic laboratory test such as a high blood sugar to confirm diabetes.

The computerized axial tomogram, a new x-ray technique that has revolutionized neurology, has helped diagnose senility in more people by showing a shrunken brain on x-ray. To get the same information in the past, doctors had to inject air into the brain, which involved not only pain but some risk to the patient. Because it is so new, the tomogram technique's usefulness in senility has not been fully explored. At present it can support the doctor's bedside impression, but it is not considered a specific diagnostic test.

Many conditions can produce symptoms that mimic senility, and many people are falsely labelled senile when their symptoms are due to depression, a thyroid gland abnormality, pernicious anemia, effects of drugs like bromides, or a variety of other conditions that can be effectively treated, if not cured, by psychotherapy or drugs.

But at most 20 percent of senility cases have a treatable cause. This situation has raised questions in the minds of some budget-conscious officials about the cost-effectiveness of spending up to $500 just for extensive series of diagnostic laboratory tests on all senile patients when they have but a few years to live.

However, the overwhelming majority of physicians would agree with Dr. Leslie Libow, chief of geriatric medicine at the Jewish Institute for Geriatric Care in New Hyde Park, who said:

"Senility is one of the most serious medical diagnoses that can be given to a patient because the prognosis is so serious and the effectiveness of treatment is not clear. If we value our older people, how can anyone seriously argue that every physician should not do the tests to make sure a treatable cause has not been overlooked?"

The older population's growing political influence has led government officials to devote more attention to their medical troubles. Next month, for example, the National Institute of Aging, the newest unit of the Federal National Institutes of Health in Bethesda, Md., will hold one of the larger scientific meetings on senility.

One impetus for the meeting is the recognition from research studies during the last five years that arteriosclerosis, or hardening of the arteries, plays less of a role in senility than doctors previously believed. Senility on the basis of arteriosclerosis tends to produce worsening symptoms on an episodic basis. Now, geriatricians believe the bulk of cases are due to senile dementia, a disease of unknown cause that occurs more commonly in women and that is characterized by the gradual, unrelenting, irreversible deterioration of the mind. The process can occur so slowly and subtly as to escape attention until the affected person shocks his family by wandering away from home, failing to recognize an old friend, or squandering money on a worthless cause.

When senility develops in a 40- or 50-year-old individual—it is then called pre-senile dementia—doctors generally suspect a wide variety of conditions, but two in particular, Alzheimer's Disease and Pick's Disease. In Alzheimer's Disease, the shrinkage occurs throughout the brain, whereas in Pick's Disease the changes are more localized. Anatomically, Alzheimer's Disease is indistinguishable from the shrunken, senile brain to the pathologist, raising questions whether Alzheimer's might be the early onset of the more common form of senility.

The main thrust of the meeting will be to explore the various avenues of research through which the mystery of senility might be solved. Among the current areas of focus:

• Epidemiology—What clues can be picked up by examining the differences in incidence among various populations that could not be detected by laboratory studies?

• Viral—Can viruses that take years to incubate and produce damage be an important cause of senility?

• Hereditary—Is there a genetic defect that predisposes some individuals to senility? If so, what is it?

• Metabolic—Is there a biochemical abnormality that leads to senility?

The answers to these and other questions could lead to effective therapies and preventions for one of society's more costly troubles.

2. Take notes on the following newspaper article. Include one note that summarizes the new theory about the apparently sudden extinction of giant mammals at the end of the last ice age. Also fill out a bibliography card for any additional source you come across as you read this article.

The topic and hypothesis with which you will be working are provided, but you will need to think of your own subtopics as you go through the article.

Topic: *Early man's relationships with other creatures*

Hypothesis: "Even in prehistoric times, man drastically altered the world around him."

New Clues to Animals Of the Ice Age

By WALTER SULLIVAN

ONE WOULD hardly expect a relationship between sea otters, crustaceans and aboriginal Aleuts to cast light on the mysterious extinctions of giant mammals at the end of the last ice age.

Scientists have reached some conclusions in that line, however, after studying the heaps of refuse left by early inhabitants of the remote Aleutian Islands.

The goal was to test the controversial hypothesis that such inhabitants of North America as the mammoth, mastodon, giant beaver, giraffelike camel and elephant-sized sloth were victims of human overkill. It has been estimated that during a few centuries, between 11,000 and 14,000 years ago, the total weight of large animals on North American soil was reduced more than 90 percent.

•

Similar extinctions occurred in other parts of the world, some suspect at times when weapons suited to big-game hunting were developed in various locales. Proponents of the human overkill explanation describe such finely chipped spearheads as "the first weapons of mass destruction."

Two reports in recent weeks have reinforced the belief that mass deaths occurred. Australian scientists have found, in an area smaller than a city block, the remains of some 10,000 extinct large animals, 90 percent of them giant kangaroos.

They died alongside what seems to have been an ancient spring about 26,000 years ago, 7,000 years after the first humans are believed to have reached that continent.

At Boney Springs, Mo., the remains of 31 giant mastodons have been found crowded into a pit no more than 33 feet wide and three feet deep. Dr. Jeffrey J. Saunders, of the Illinois State Museum in Springfield, said the animals died about 13,500 years ago. They, too, seem to have been at an ancient spring.

•

Those who doubt that man was to blame question whether hunters could have been responsible for such wholesale deaths. They cite the absence of human artifacts at such graveyards as those in Australia and Missouri.

A more plausible explanation, they believe, is some form of catastrophic environmental change. Dr. Saunders suspects a prolonged drought.

Members of the overkill school, such as Dr. Paul S. Martin of the University of Arizona, point out, however, that the animals survived a series of radical climate changes throughout the ice ages.

Why, these scientists ask, did the beasts die when the climate was improving, unless it was related to the presence of human hunters?

The Aleutian researchers have found evidence that, they believe, shows early hunters could have been responsible. "Contrary to popular opinion," they report in a recent issue of the journal Science, "it is likely that aboriginal man directly caused the extinction of certain New World megafauna."

•

Their conclusions are derived largely from excavations conducted on Amchitka Island, site of the high-yield underground nuclear tests, and financed by the Atomic Energy Commission.

Researchers dug through layer after layer of debris at a site occupied by

Aleuts (who are similar to, but distinct from, the Eskimos) from their arrival 2,500 years ago until the appearance of European fur hunters.

Bones in the lowest layer show that sea otters at first were a staple of the Aleut diet. But soon these animals disappeared and the Aleuts turned to sea urchins and various shellfish. Inshore fish also became rare.

The proposed explanation is that sea otters were hunted to the vanishing point, eliminating the "keystone" of the ecology.

Sea otters live on sea urchins, limpets and chitons that, in turn, eat kelp and other algae.

Today, on Aleutian islands with no otters, sea urchins carpet the shores, which are barren of kelp. Fish dependent on kelp debris for their food are also scarce. The role of the sea otter is keeping down the sea urchin population, thus allowing kelp and fish to thrive. Unfortunately the otters also enjoy abalone, competing with fishermen who harvest those shellfish.

The Amchitka excavations have shown that after otters were eliminated, the urchins became unusually large. Then, in the last centuries before arrival of Russian and American hunters, otters reappeared on the Aleut menu, possibly because the native hunters ventured farther afield.

•

The authors of the report are Charles A. Simenstad of the University of Washington, Dr. James A. Estes of the United States Fish and Wildlife Service and Karl W. Kenyon, a sea otter specialist who has retired from the service. They take issue with an earlier analysis growing out of Soviet-American investigations.

The studies, conducted on Umnak Island 500 miles east of Amchitka, were described in 1975 by William S. Laughlin of the University of Connecticut. He concluded that the aboriginal Aleuts were a "classic example" of man as a stabilizing, rather than disruptive, influence.

Although disappearance of the large ice age mammals was recent—it occurred long after Cro-Magnon man began depicting them in cave paintings— the events remain more mysterious than far earlier extinctions, such as those of the dinosaurs. The latter died out over millions of years as continental drift produced radical changes in geography, climate and environment.

6

Preparing to Write the Paper

You are now ready to enter the writing phase of the assignment since you have completed virtually all the research and reading of sources. Of course, you may have to go back and reexamine one or more sources to find information you suspect you have missed. Or you may hear of a potential source and want to check it out after you have started to write your paper. Research is seldom a straightforward process; retracing steps is frequently necessary.

The writing of a research paper is complicated by the large amount of information, often quite technical, which must be organized into a logical sequence. In order to cope with this complexity, you must first review all your findings to determine just what your investigation has accomplished. Only when you have a clear overview of your materials can you expect to be able to organize them into an effective paper.

Sorting Your Note Cards

One way to obtain such an overview is by laying all your note cards out on a table and arranging them into groups according to subtopics. (Here you can readily see the advantage to having each note on its own card so that it can be easily shifted from one group to another or from one place to another in your plan for the paper.) A review of the information contained on these cards can provide an overall sense of what your research has uncovered. From this review you should be able to establish the thesis for your paper and to begin to see, at least in a general way, how the various pieces of information might fit together to form a coherent paper.

It is not possible to say how many subtopics you will arrive at during your research, but you can usually expect to see between ten and twenty piles of note cards lying before you. After reviewing the full set of notes, you should consolidate the small piles under a few fairly broad subtopics so that you can make a rough outline—the backbone of your paper. For his Jefferson Davis paper, the student took the cards that he had assigned to various subtopics—vision of South's greatness, previous administrative experience, service as United States senator, achievements as army officer, views on individual liberty, convictions about states' rights—and put them in one pile forming the major subtopic, Davis's strong points. Later, when constructing his detailed outline for the paper, he reduced this broad subtopic to three headings: Davis's vision of the South's potential greatness, Davis's integrity and political convictions, and Davis's military and government experience.

By looking through your stacks of note cards, you must try to determine whether your investigation of the topic is complete. If you feel you do not have enough evidence from which to draw a definite conclusion, you need to do more research: either find more sources or get more information from the sources you have already examined. Even if you feel confident of the conclusion you have reached, you still need to ask whether the research has been thorough. For a paper on dinosaur extinction, for instance, you may have taken just one brief note about a particular theory that is not widely held. For the research to be complete, you must take time to find a more detailed account of that theory so that you can evaluate it for the readers of your paper.

Asking Yourself Questions to Determine Your Thesis

Imagine, now, that you are not an author planning to write a paper but a consultant called in by the author to decide whether it is wise to move ahead to the writing stage. As a consultant, your objective is to judge whether the research has been thorough and to evaluate the hypothesis. If the hypothesis accurately reflects the overall picture delineated by the research, it can serve as the paper's thesis.

When serving as your own consultant, be as objective as a real consultant would be. Do not accept answers without a satisfactory explanation of how they were arrived at. Be especially tough-minded when evaluating the accuracy of the hypothesis.

The following set of questions and answers might have taken place in the head of the student who wrote the paper on Jefferson Davis.

Question: What was your purpose in doing this research?

Answer: I had to prepare a paper for a course in nineteenth-century American history. I took *Davis* as a topic because I had heard that he was a poor leader and I wanted to know where he had gone wrong. When my preliminary research indicated he might not have been as weak as I had believed, I decided to learn how good or bad he really was.

Question: What did your research reveal?

Answer: Although his personal faults led him to make some mistakes, Davis was basically a good leader. His failings were probably no greater than Lincoln's, but since the South lost, Davis became the scapegoat, and Lincoln was idealized.

Question: How did you find this out?

Answer: I read several biographies of Davis and some major studies of the Civil War that commented extensively on Davis.

Question: Did they all agree on Davis's performance as president of the Confederacy?

Answer: They didn't agree at all. One blamed him entirely for the South's defeat; another regarded him as a tragic martyr. Several recent works recognized both his faults and his strengths and concluded that the good outweighed the bad.

Question: How did you decide which view to accept?

Answer: The most recent writers offered more evidence to go on, and I thought their arguments were stronger than those attacking Davis.

Question: But you said that Davis made some serious mistakes. How can you discount the low opinion of the man which so many historians held for so long?

Answer: Sure, Davis made mistakes. He became too involved with administrative details, and he entered into personal battles with other Confederate leaders. He also tried to influence military decisions which rightly belonged to the generals. Still, he came to the job with outstanding qualifications, and he accomplished a great deal in spite of his shortcomings. Earlier writers weren't necessarily wrong in their evaluation of Davis, except for one who knew Davis personally and hated him. They based their judgments on the evidence, but they probably used too high a standard in making those judgments. When compared objectively with Lincoln, who also interfered in military matters and at times acted in an authoritarian and maybe even unconstitutional way, Davis comes off pretty well. The real question seems to be: How high a standard should be used to judge a leader?

Question: All this about Lincoln may be true, but weren't there other talented Southerners who would have done better or at least made fewer errors?

Answer: I thought so when I was doing the preliminary reading. But from my research, and from what I know in general about leaders and politicians, I'd say that the other candidates would surely have been handicapped by their personal problems or character flaws. Even Robert E. Lee, who attained truly heroic stature in the eyes of history, had some serious faults. Jefferson Davis's faults are plain to see, but I do not believe that they could have caused the South's defeat. Besides, Davis's enemies would have given anyone else in his position just as much trouble, given the serious philosophical and practical disagreements among the secessionists.

At this point, the student might have summarized his self-questioning:

> I originally thought that Davis was largely responsible for the South's defeat, but my research has shown that hypothesis to be inaccurate. It now seems reasonable to accept the position that Davis was a talented leader facing an impossible situation. Historians had previously underrated him because of some personal failings and because the South lost the war.
>
> My thesis would therefore run something like this: "Although until recently most historians have been highly critical of Jefferson Davis's performance as president of the Confederacy, he was actually a very talented leader, perhaps the best man available for the job."

The Introductory Paragraph

After you have settled on your thesis and assured yourself that you have done a thorough job of research, the next step is to write an introductory paragraph for your paper. This paragraph not only states your thesis, but also indicates the major subtopics within the paper and describes the general nature of your sources. It therefore goes hand in hand with constructing the outline. Writing a draft of your introductory or thesis paragraph before constructing your outline might appear unorthodox, but it offers a significant advantage: a paragraph that introduces your major subtopics in the order in which you plan to deal with them gives you a good "feel" for the paper as a whole. It can also serve as a convenient guide as you write the balance of the paper.

Before writing the introductory paragraph, you should jot down the major points you expect it to include. For the paper on Davis, these main points were:

Topic: Jefferson Davis's leadership of the Confederacy

Subtopics: comparison to Lincoln; problems with other leaders; overwork and poor health; personal strengths; South's hopeless situation

Sources: biographies and historical studies, from just after the war to now; emphasis on recent works

From these items, the student prepared a rough draft of his introductory paragraph:

topic	For a long time, historians have blamed Davis for the South's loss of the Civil War.
subtopic	But a modern writer compared Davis to Lincoln and showed that Lincoln also made serious mistakes and had as many faults. Of course, the North won, so Lincoln became a hero and
thesis (brief)	Davis a scapegoat. Some writers today see Davis as a very able leader faced with an impossible task. To be sure, Davis had his
subtopic	faults. Having been a successful army officer, he often tried to run the fighting of the war, angering the generals and causing confusion.
subtopic	He also fought bitterly with several political opponents, creating needless tension and
subtopic	confusing issues. As for administration itself, he spent too much time on details, and
sources	his weak health suffered. Older writers on Davis and the war felt these character faults contributed a great deal to the loss of the
thesis	war. Some recent writers, however, having more evidence to work with plus a fresh approach, have found Davis a first-rate leader in spite of his personality problems.

This paragraph needs polishing, but it fulfills the basic aims of an introductory paragraph—it gives readers a clear idea of what the writer is trying to do and how he means to do it. The final version, which follows, was not produced until the rest of the paper had been written. Note in particular the structural changes. The thesis is stated just once, at the end of the paragraph where it carries the most weight. The addition of a quotation from one of the sources provides a nice touch. Finally, several of the subtopics are presented in more general terms so that readers will not be distracted by the details.

      For many years after Robert E. Lee surrendered at Appomattox, historians tended to lay much of the blame for the South's crushing defeat upon the president of the Confederacy, Jefferson Davis. However, one writer, in comparing Davis to Lincoln, claims that Davis's reputation would have been quite different if he had been on the winning side. When a leader fails to achieve victory, even if his cause was doomed from the start, his "errors and defects and limitations of character . . . stand out as do a few spots of ink on a white sheet of paper."[1] This does not mean that Davis had no faults. Almost all historians agree that the man suffered from character flaws. He spent far too much time on administrative details, he often interfered in purely military matters, and he allowed himself to be drawn into bitter controversies with other political leaders. The question all Civil War analysts must answer is: To what extent did Davis's failings contribute to the defeat of the Confederacy? A survey of modern studies of Davis and the Civil War reveals a softening in the historical judgment of Davis as a leader. Most historians today conclude that Jefferson Davis, despite his personal shortcomings, was probably the most capable president the South could have chosen. Indeed, given the enormous problems the Confederacy faced, Davis was a definite asset in the struggle to secede from the Union.

main subtopics

nature of sources

thesis statement

Outlining

Once you have drafted your introductory paragraph, your next concern is the structure of the paper. An outline is essential if you expect to control all the information that lies spread out on the table before you. Outlining can be done in several stages, culminating in a detailed plan for the paper, in which each note card has been assigned its appropriate place. (Examples of such an outline are included with the sample research papers in Chapter 9.)

Your first outline for a paper can be very simple—just take your major subtopics and figure out a reasonable order in which to present them. The original plan for the Jefferson Davis paper looked like this:

Introductory paragraph

1. Davis's strengths—why he was chosen
2. Davis's weaknesses—why he has been criticized
3. The traditional view of Davis—emphasis on faults
4. The latest assessment of his leadership—the best man available
5. Comparison with Lincoln
   Conclusion

A brief outline such as this gives you a chance to think about the shape of the paper without being confused by all the details you have collected in your research. Next, you should mark down these sources that go with each proposed section, in order to see how well you are utilizing your major sources. In this example, the third item seems likely to repeat the second one to a large extent, so revision is required. The revised brief outline, on which the complete final outline was based, follows:

Introductory paragraph

1. Davis's weaknesses—the traditional view (Pollard)
2. Davis's strengths—why he was chosen (Strode)
3. Two moderate views (Nevins; Randall and Donald)
4. Defense of Davis based on the South's problems (Catton)
5. Davis's weaknesses compared with Lincoln's (Barney; Rabun)
   Conclusion

The next stage, constructing a detailed outline, depends on a careful evaluation of your materials. First, arrange the piles of note cards in the same order as the subtopics in your brief outline. Then, read through your notes again, to be sure they are both relevant and usable. You may want to eliminate a note that no longer seems as relevant as it did when you wrote it, to reassign a minor subtopic to a different major subtopic, or perhaps even to return to the library and look for information on an important subtopic about which you have not uncovered enough information.

Now you are ready to put your full set of cards in the precise order you expect to follow when writing the paper. Start by arranging the minor subtopics within the major subtopic to which you have assigned them. Then, arrange all the note cards within each minor subtopic in a logical sequence. By arranging your entire collection of notes in this way, you will have laid out on the table an organizational pattern for your paper. This is, in effect, a physical outline, and from it you can prepare the detailed written outline that will guide your writing of the first draft.

THE MATTER OF BALANCE

As you put your groups of note cards into sequence, look for possible imbalance. No subtopic should outweigh or overshadow other equally important subtopics. For example, suppose you were writing about Martin Luther King, Jr., and had arrived at the thesis, "Martin Luther King's success resulted from three major factors—his courage, his intelligence, and his charisma." Your outline, which determines the shape of the paper, would be unbalanced if you devoted one section to "courage," one to "intelligence," and then six sections to "charisma." If your general impression from reading the sources was that all three factors contributed equally to King's success, then you would need to return to your sources or find additional sources for more information about the two briefly covered factors. If, however, you now realize that most of the sources had indeed emphasized charisma, you must recast your thesis. It might well read, "Martin Luther King's success depended on three factors—courage, intelligence, and charisma—of which charisma was by far the most important." Whatever direction you take, be sure to correct an unbalanced outline before you start to write. You will find it much harder to do so later.

THE OUTLINE FORMAT

In constructing an outline, you can use whatever format you feel comfortable with, unless your instructor requires you to use a particular format. One of the most common formats uses a combination of letters and numbers to designate the various levels of classification. Even if you are already familiar with this format, take time to be sure you understand the subtle distinctions between those levels.

This list indicates the relative difference between levels:

Roman numerals (I, II) represent major subtopics, usually covering a large section of the paper.

Capital letters (A, B) represent minor subtopics, often discussed in several paragraphs.

Arabic numerals (1, 2) represent major details that support a minor subtopic.

Small letters (a, b) represent minor details that support a major detail.

The longer the paper you are writing, the broader the area covered by the highest category (Roman numerals) and the greater the chance that you might need a fifth set of symbols to represent the smallest details in the paper (small Roman numerals—i, ii, iii).

Notice the use of these levels of classification in the following segment of the outline for the Davis paper. (This kind of outline is sometimes called a phrase outline because each entry in it is a phrase rather than a sentence.)

<table>
<tr><td></td><td>Introductory paragraph, including the thesis statement</td></tr>
<tr><td>major subtopic</td><td>I. Extreme views of Davis's leadership</td></tr>
<tr><td>minor subtopic</td><td> A. Negative (Pollard)</td></tr>
<tr><td>major detail</td><td>   1. Responsibility for loss of the war</td></tr>
<tr><td>minor details</td><td>   a. Squandering of South's resources</td></tr>
<tr><td></td><td>   b. An "imbecile and barren" administration</td></tr>
<tr><td></td><td>   c. Personal vanity</td></tr>
<tr><td>major detail</td><td>   2. Pollard's bias</td></tr>
<tr><td>minor details</td><td>   a. Personal dislike of Davis</td></tr>
<tr><td></td><td>   b. Need for a scapegoat (Patrick)</td></tr>
<tr><td>minor subtopic</td><td> B. Positive (Strode)</td></tr>
<tr><td>major detail</td><td>   1. Davis's strengths</td></tr>
<tr><td>minor details</td><td>   a. Unselfishness and integrity</td></tr>
<tr><td></td><td>   b. Minor nature of his flaws</td></tr>
<tr><td></td><td>   c. Refusal to play politics at expense of civil liberties</td></tr>
<tr><td>major detail</td><td>   2. Superiority to Lincoln in regard to civil liberties</td></tr>
<tr><td>minor details</td><td>   a. Implied comparison</td></tr>
<tr><td></td><td>   b. Direct comparison (Dodd)</td></tr>
<tr><td>major detail</td><td>   3. Nobility of Davis in a doomed cause</td></tr>
</table>

Your instructor may want you to follow two rules for the outline format.

Rule 1: *Never break a category down into just one subdivision. To do so is illogical.*

wrong; only one
detail supports the
subtopic

```
I.  Difficulties faced by Diego Rivera in
    early years
    A.  Childhood problems
        1.  Grave illness from typhus and
            scarlet fever
    B.  Adolescent problems
```

At some point, childhood problems must have seemed an important subtopic, but in this outline it looks trivial. Perhaps a note on another childhood problem has been assigned to another subtopic and could be moved into this one. Or perhaps another trip to the library would produce details about a second childhood problem accidentally omitted during note-taking. The outline might then look like this:

correct

```
I.  Difficulties faced by Diego Rivera in
    early years
    A.  Childhood problems
        1.  Grave illness from typhus and
            scarlet fever
        2.  Dangers arising from father's
            radical politics
    B.  Adolescent problems
```

On the other hand, if Rivera's only significant childhood problem had been illness, the outline might be revised to look like this:

correct

```
I.  Difficulties faced by Diego Rivera in
    early years
    A.  Childhood illnesses
    B.  Adolescent problems
```

(It is not necessary to add arabic numerals under *A* for the specific illnesses, unless your note cards treat them extensively and you mean to discuss them in detail.)

Rule 2: *Use the same grammatical form for words at the same level of classification. By doing so, you produce parallel structure, that is, a logical and symmetrical ordering of ideas.*

wrong; the subdivisions are not grammatically parallel	A. Symptoms of senility
	    1. Forgetting recent events
	    2. Mistakes in simple arithmetic
	    3. Occasional hallucinating
	    4. Inappropriate responses in social situations

correct; each subdivision is a gerund phrase	A. Symptoms of senility
	    1. Forgetting recent events
	    2. Making mistakes in simple arithmetic
	    3. Hallucinating occasionally
	    4. Responding inappropriately in social situations

SENTENCE OUTLINES

Some instructors may require you to submit a *sentence outline,* in which you must present your information in complete sentences. A sentence outline usually takes more time to write than a phrase outline, but it offers you the advantage of putting your information down in a form that can often be used almost word for word when you start to write your full paper. Whatever kind of outline you prepare, be consistent. Do not mix phrases into a sentence outline or sentences into a phrase outline.

Here is a sample section from a sentence outline:

complete sentences appear at each level of entry	A. Diego Rivera suffered from a number of childhood problems.
	    1. Rivera contracted typhus at nine and nearly died from scarlet fever at eleven.
	    2. Rivera faced dangers resulting from his father's radical politics.

A FINAL WORD ON OUTLINING

The major reason for constructing an outline is to organize your thoughts and notes into a logical pattern before you write your research paper. It may happen that the classification levels and their accompanying numbers and letters refuse to fall neatly into place, even after several attempts. If, however, you are sure that your outline is a logical plan for organizing your paper from thesis statement to conclusion, then you have satisfied the most important requirement of the outline assignment. Your instructor can easily offer you suggestions for fitting your outline into the traditional format and using the proper symbols (I, A, 1, a).

Review Questions

1. Why do you review and arrange all your note cards before you begin any writing? What problems might you discover at this stage and how might you deal with them?
2. How do you determine the thesis of your paper?
3. What are the usual objectives of an introductory paragraph?
4. What is the function of an outline? What are some problems that you might encounter in constructing an outline?

Exercise

Read the following introductory paragraphs, keeping in mind that such a paragraph should state the thesis, identify the major subtopics for the paper, and describe the general nature of the sources used. Which paragraph best fulfills these objectives? Explain your choice.

Topic: *Emily Dickinson's reluctance to publish her poems*

VERSION 1

Emily Dickinson was born in Amherst, Massachusetts, on December 10, 1830. She was the second of three children born to Edward and Emily Dickinson. She had an older brother, Austin, who was born on April 16, 1829. Her sister, Lavinia, was born on February 28, 1833. "The three children were devoted to one another, but their home did not provoke gaiety."[1] Dickinson went to school at Amherst Academy, and later spent a term at Mount Holyoke College. According to Clark Griffith, in 1858 "she began definitely and noticeably to seclude herself from the outside world."[2] With rare exceptions, she spent the rest of her life in her father's house in Amherst. Emily Dickinson died in 1886, leaving behind her over 1700 poems. Only seven of her poems were published while she was alive, and all of these were published

anonymously.[3] Today she is considered to be a great poet. During
her lifetime, however, she was reluctant to publish, and many
people have wondered why.

VERSION 2

Great poets are never appreciated during their lifetimes.
Emily Dickinson was a great poet. Yvor Winters, in fact, called
her "one of the great lyric poets of all time."[1] Actually, she
was so far ahead of her time that she could not be appreciated
while she was alive. Only seven of her more than 1700 poems were
published during her lifetime, and even these appeared
anonymously.[2] Why should any poet try to become famous if fame
means that she has to change her poems to conform to the
unimaginative poetic standards of her day? To be a great poet
requires great confidence in one's artistic ability.
Unfortunately, the public is always too tradition-bound to
recognize true art when it appears in an unfamiliar form. Emily
Dickinson's work is no exception. The question is: Are there any
Emily Dickinsons today whose brilliance remains unappreciated
due to our cultural blindness?

VERSION 3

Emily Dickinson, one of America's greatest poets, was all but
unknown during her lifetime, for she allowed only a handful of
her more than 1700 poems to be published, and these appeared
anonymously. Only after her death were her works discovered by
her sister and brought forth to a warm public reception. Ever
since then, the many persons who have written about this unusual
genius have attempted to explain her reluctance to publish. The
image created by literary critics and popular historians alike
is that of a shy, reclusive, mystical dreamer—a sensitive soul
deeply wrapped up in her personal joys and sorrows. However, a
new picture of the poet has come forth from scholars working
closely with her correspondence and with fresh biographical
evidence. This view reveals an artist who felt sure of her own
worth and chose deliberately to keep her creations from a world
she believed incapable of understanding them and insensitive to
their aesthetic value. Those brilliant poems would lie safely in
her desk until they could be appreciated properly, even at the
expense of public recognition.

7

Writing the Paper

After you have developed a logical outline and written an introductory paragraph, you are ready to write the paper itself. This task will consume a good deal of time, since you must plan to write at least three versions of your paper: a rough draft, a revised draft, and a polished final manuscript suitable for submission to your instructor. Many writers feel the need for even further revision, but three drafts are the absolute minimum.

Writing the Rough Draft

Writing the rough draft of a research paper can be thought of as "filling in the outline" because the outline provides a structure not just for your own ideas and conclusions but for the many research notes you have taken. If you try to write your rough draft by working only from the note cards, it will be much harder for you to keep in mind the relationships among them. Worst of all is trying to write the draft from memory, off the top of your head. That approach may work well for writing essays based on personal experience, but if used for a research paper it absolutely guarantees mistakes and omissions.

When writing the rough draft, you may think of a better way to present your case than you had planned. Should you find yourself in this situation, resist the temptation to be lazy: revise your outline or even construct a new one. Remember that if you change part of your outline, you may have to change other parts as well in order to maintain balance and an orderly and logical presentation of ideas.

Since the first draft is not meant to be seen by anyone but yourself, don't try to get every sentence or word into perfect form. Try to express yourself clearly. If you can't, the chances are that you need to think more about what you are trying to say. On the other hand, do not worry if the best possible wording escapes you at the moment, and especially do not worry about spelling and punctuation. Let your ideas and sentences flow as freely as you can, getting everything down on paper in a form which reflects your thinking, however roughly. When you write the second draft, finding the right words for what you want to say may be considerably easier.

Here are three pieces of advice for the format of the first draft. First, leave plenty of space between the lines for later insertions and changes—about two lines of space for every line of writing. Second, don't slow yourself down by copying out each quotation, paraphrase, or summary from your cards. When you come to a place where you need to use a note, simply make a memo to yourself that says "copy from card" or "see card." Or, before you start writing, you might take all of your note cards to a copy center or to the copying machine in the library and make photocopies. You can then cut and paste these copies right into the draft. Finally, be sure to note briefly in the margin the source of each note you use in the paper, no matter if it is a direct quotation, a paraphrase, or a summary. You can simply note the author's name or a key word or two from the title. If you fail to make a note, you may later forget to add a source footnote.

You have already begun your first draft by writing an introductory paragraph that states your thesis and mentions the major points you intend to make. The body of the paper will deal at length with the subtopics in your outline.

How does one "fill in the outline"? This aspect of the process is not just a matter of mentioning the subtopics and copying down the notes that go with each one. Rather, you are expected to write an essay on the topic, presenting and defending your thesis, using your note cards to remind you of the details that serve as evidence to support your argument. The same standards of coherence, reasoning, and style that apply to other kinds of writing apply to research papers as well.

INTEGRATING YOUR SOURCES

Though you are by now familiar with your notes, you are for the first time trying to blend them into a coherent whole. Certain situations may arise as you are writing the first draft and cause special kinds of problems. The following three problems occur fairly frequently.

No one source tells the whole story. Often you will have to draw details from different sources in order to deal with a subtopic as fully as you need to. This is perfectly all right to do, but you must be careful to keep track of which facts come from which sources. If you simply combine all the details into one account of the situation, without source notes, your readers may not realize what you had to do to put the picture together.

Several sources disagree over a question of fact. Here you have several options. You may simply report the disagreement, especially if you have no basis for trusting one source more than the others. Or you may decide that one source is indeed more trustworthy than the others—more fully documented, more exhaustive, or more recent—and choose its version of the fact. Or you can try to verify the fact by further research. (The student writing about Emily Dickinson found that various sources said the number of poems published during the poet's lifetime was six, seven, or eight. Since the source that was most exhaustive and best documented said the number was seven, the student simply used that number in her paper and disregarded the other sources' claims. She did so because she was in no position to verify the fact herself. Her library did not have an extensive file of the New England periodicals in which Dickinson's poems might have appeared, and, even had the sources been available, the student did not have the time to search through hundreds of periodicals looking for anonymously published Dickinson poems. She did not reveal the discrepancy among her sources in her paper because it was simply not important to her thesis.)

Different sources disagree in their interpretation of a fact or facts. Such differences occur all the time; in fact, they are among the things that make research interesting. If the purpose of your paper is not to argue for a particular conclusion but to report the current state of knowledge, you may simply report the disagreement. If, however, your thesis states a definite position regarding your topic, you must not only report the disagreement but draw your own conclusion as to which interpretation seems more soundly argued or based on more complete or more reliable evidence. In reporting the disagreement, you must be fair to the writers whose interpretations you reject by presenting their views with enough detail that your readers can decide whether or not to agree with your preference.

As you can see, writing the first draft involves a great deal of thinking about the ideas and information in your notes in order to draw reasonable conclusions about them. It is this thinking, and not the physical act of writing down your thoughts or keeping track of your sources, that makes the first draft a time-consuming and challenging task. This is also why we encourage you not to get bogged down trying to express your thoughts in exactly the right words. You have enough to do without worrying about that.

When the body of your paper is complete, you must compose a suitable conclusion. As a general rule, the conclusion should not introduce any new ideas or information. Instead, it should restate your thesis in terms that reflect the evidence that you have presented. (If you use the same words that you used to state your thesis in your introduction, your readers may feel that you haven't taken them anywhere.) Above all, your conclusion should bring your paper to a satisfying close with a statement that sums up what you think your research has shown. Don't be afraid to commit yourself in this respect: you ought to be able to stand confidently behind your research.

Now that you have completed a first draft of your paper, set the project aside for at least a few hours and do something else. It would be best if you could take at least a day's vacation. During the time you are not consciously working at the research project, your unconscious mind will be digesting, synthesizing, and generally working with what you have done. Then, as you tackle the second draft, not only will you feel refreshed, but you may also find yourself brimming with new ideas.

Revising the Rough Draft

Once you have brought your outline to life by writing a rough essay, the nature of your job changes significantly. You must now become your own toughest critic. Read what you have written closely, as if for the first time, so that you can find those parts which communicate most effectively as well as those which work poorly or not at all. Then you can become the author again, rewriting and, if necessary, reorganizing the weaker passages so that they become as strong as the best. Finally, you must examine the revised essay very closely in order to correct the spelling, punctuation, and other mechanical details.

Approach your revision in an orderly way, by thinking of the task on four levels of organization: the whole paper, paragraphs, sentences, and individual words and phrases. First, reconsider the order of the major and minor subtopics as presented in your outline and see if it still serves your purposes well.

Once you are satisfied that these larger elements of the paper have been presented in an effective sequence, reexamine the structure of each paragraph and revise where necessary. Then look for sentences that could use improvement. Long, cumbersome sentences, for example, can be broken down into simpler, more easily digested units, but sometimes your revision will work in the other direction—combining a series of short, choppy sentences into longer, smoothly flowing sentences. Still other sentences must simply be recast to make them clearer. Finally, read through the paper, checking your transitions between paragraphs and the details within each paragraph.

Changes in wording can be made at any stage of your revision, even when you are repairing weak paragraph organization or faulty sentence structure. But you should still give yourself one last chance to improve your choice of words just before writing the final, polished version.

RECONSIDERING THE ORGANIZATION

As you constructed your outline and arranged your note cards, you considered at some length the best order in which to present the information and ideas that would go into your argument for your thesis. Writing the first draft, however, you might have felt that your plan was not completely practical. Rereading your draft you may be more dissatisfied than ever. What can you do?

Perhaps you decided when constructing the outline to present the evidence in support of your thesis first and the evidence against it afterwards. This strategy is effective if your case is so strong that it will make the opposing arguments seem weak. On rereading your paper, however, you found that the opposing case did not seem weak; instead, it seemed to rebut much of your case point by point. One way to reverse that effect would be to switch the order of those subtopics, stating the opposing case first and rebutting it with your case. At this stage of the revision, you would not need to do any rewriting. You would simply cut the two passages out of the paper and tape or paste them back in the new order. Later you would rewrite them and revise the transitions to make the new order effective.

The same strategy would work if you needed to rearrange minor subtopics or individual paragraphs. Suppose, for example, that you had arranged a series of minor subtopics to put the strongest point first and to end with the weakest, but on rereading your first draft you thought that this arrangement caused an anticlimax. You would snip the paragraphs out of the paper and shift them into a new order.

Rearrangements of this kind might require more revision than simple adjustments in paragraph or sentence structure: you might occasionally find it a good idea to rewrite drastically rearranged parts of the paper to produce a new "first" draft to work with. More often, however, you will find your outline a good guide and no major reorganization necessary. You can then go on to revising the individual paragraphs.

REVISING PARAGRAPHS

Think of a paragraph as a group of sentences that work together to support a controlling idea—the idea expressed in the *topic* (or *main idea*) *sentence*. Ask yourself if a reader would be able to grasp without difficulty the controlling ideas in your paragraphs, either because you have provided clear topic sentences or because you have so carefully constructed your paragraphs that the controlling ideas can be inferred readily from all the sentences taken together. Although you should not feel that you must impose a single rigid concept of paragraph structure on your writing, you should be certain that your paragraphs contribute to a logical progression of ideas in your paper. To the extent that they do not, you must revise.

If you think that one or more of your paragraphs might be confusing to a reader, the first thing to do is to see if the rewriting (or inclusion) of a topic sentence will clarify your thoughts. If a paragraph remains confusing even after you have improved its topic sentence or created a new topic sentence for it, you must focus on two additional features of paragraph structure:

1. the order in which you have presented the details in support of your topic sentence
2. the smoothness with which you have moved from one sentence to the next or from one idea to another

As you review your work, try to read each paragraph as though you were a reader unaware of what the writer intended to say. Check the order of the details by rearranging them until you have found the most effective order for them. If the progression from one detail to the next is not smooth, take your composition book or rhetoric and read about achieving coherence, or logical sequence, in paragraphs. Pay special attention to what the book says about using transitional words and phrases and other devices for linking ideas smoothly and logically. A short review of this kind can enable you to improve the flow of thought within your paragraphs and throughout your paper as a whole.

REVISING SENTENCES

Writing effective sentences is primarily a matter of style, and style can be developed only through a great deal of practice. Even when you recognize that a sentence calls for improvement, you may have trouble deciding just what changes would make it better. As you revise your paper, you can help yourself by being alert to a few common weaknesses in sentence construction. Pay particular attention to sentences in your rough draft that may be too complex or too simple and to patterns of construction that may be monotonously repetitive.

First, check the length of your sentences. Some may be too long and complicated for readers to follow comfortably. Usually such sentences can be broken down into more easily digested sentences, as the examples illustrate.

too long a sentence

Throughout the war, many Southerners came to think of Lincoln as a power—hungry autocrat, who, in spite of the public speeches in which he advocated peace and reconciliation, was in reality determined to destroy anyone, in the North or South, who stood in the way of his gaining absolute control of the nation he had been elected to govern.

improvement

Throughout the war, many Southerners came to think of Lincoln as a power—hungry autocrat, in spite of the public speeches in which he advocated peace and reconciliation. They believed that he was in reality determined to destroy anyone, in the North or South, who stood in the way of his gaining absolute control of the nation he had been elected to govern.

Short sentences are easy to understand, but a series of five or six very short, choppy sentences actually may be more difficult to read than two or three sentences of average length. When you find such a series in your draft, consider combining several of them into longer sentences. Save your short sentences until they can be used most effectively—for example, when emphasizing or summing up a particularly important point.

too many short sentences

Throughout the war, many people detested Lincoln. They considered him to be power—hungry. His speeches called for peace and reconciliation. But these people did not believe him. They included Northerners as well as Southerners. They believed that he intended to destroy anyone who opposed him. They

thought he desired to gain absolute control of
the country. They saw his election as part of
his plan to rule as a dictator.

improvement   Throughout the war, many people detested
Lincoln, whom they considered power-hungry.
Although his speeches called for peace and
reconciliation, these people did not believe
him. Both Northerners and Southerners thought
that he intended to destroy anyone who opposed
him and sought dictatorial control of the
country he had been elected to govern.

Also check the patterns of your sentences to see if you have repeated one pattern monotonously. Such repetition may needlessly bore your readers.

repetitive pattern   Hartman says that . . . Anna Freud states that
. . . Mahler claims that . . . And now Kohut
states that . . .

improvement   Hartman says that . . . Further support comes
from Anna Freud . . . Mahler agrees, for the
most part, claiming that . . . Recently, Kohut
added further support to this idea when he
stated . . .

The second example is an improvement over the first not only because it is more varied but also because the writer has taken a set of ideas from different sources and blended them into a smoothly flowing passage that shows how these ideas relate to each other.

REVISING WORD CHOICE

When you revise your word choice, there are three elements you should keep in mind:

1. *variety*—finding appropriate synonyms for words that appear often, except for technical terms which do not allow substitutes
2. *accuracy*—avoiding vague, loose terms that may be misinterpreted
3. *slang*—avoiding words that are not appropriate to the formal context of a research paper

This example illustrates the need for *variety:*

lacking variety

A young, idealistic anthropologist, on first venturing into a primitive society, is likely to suffer severe disillusionment. For one thing, most such societies live under physical conditions that no one coming from American society can possibly anticipate. But far more dispiriting is the fact that these societies often practice customs radically opposite to the ideal life in nature that naive students like to imagine: a society of simple folk, yes, but a society that knows the true value of love, kindness, sharing, and mutual respect. The Yanomamo society provides an example that could try the soul of any young idealist searching for simple, natural virtues. Their social practices include . . .

improvement

A young, idealistic anthropologist, on first venturing into a primitive society, is likely to suffer severe disillusionment. For one thing, most such people live under physical conditions that no one coming from America can possibly anticipate. But far more dispiriting is the fact that these communities often practice customs radically opposite to the ideal life in nature that naive students like to imagine: a society of simple folk, yes, but one that knows the true value of love, kindness, sharing, and mutual respect. The Yanomamo tribe provides an example that could try the soul of any young idealist searching for simple, natural virtues. Their social practices include . . .

Here are some examples illustrating the emptiness of vague words:

vague

Napoleon was a great man.
Sarah Bernhardt was a great actress.
Einstein was a great thinker.
Oedipus Rex is a great play.

improved
            Napoleon was an outstanding military
                strategist.
            Sarah Bernhardt played a wide variety of roles
                to perfection.
            Einstein's theories reshaped the world of
                modern physics.
            The play Oedipus Rex provides meaningful
                insights into human behavior.

Of course, you cannot entirely avoid vague terms, but you can keep them to a minimum and use them with care. In short, say exactly what you mean, or at least come as close as possible.

The following are examples of word choices not appropriate to the formal context of a research paper:

inappropriate
            The women in Rubens's paintings are very sexy.
            The FBI has been blasted recently for failing
                to perform its duties with sufficient
                restraint.
            The prosecutor called upon a well-known shrink
                to testify that the defendant was not
                legally crazy.

improved
            The women in Rubens's paintings are very
                sensuous.
            The FBI has been sharply criticized recently
                for failing to perform its duties with
                sufficient restraint.
            The prosecutor called upon a well-known
                psychiatrist to testify that the
                defendant was not legally insane.

When revising word choice, be careful if you decide to use a *thesaurus,* or collection of synonyms. Books of synonyms can be valuable in helping you to remember a word whose meaning you know well; they can be dangerous if you use them to select high-sounding words that are unfamiliar to you. The connotations of such words may not be appropriate to the contexts in which you place them. You may find a *dictionary of synonyms* more useful than a thesaurus because the former defines and illustrates the different shades of meaning between synonyms.

Writing the Polished, Final Draft

Equipped with a carefully revised draft, you are ready to produce the polished, final version of your research paper. As you write the final version, you may continue to make changes in wording to improve the clarity of your paper. You may also make minor alterations in your paragraphs and sentences in order to improve the flow of thought. However, if at this time you find yourself making major changes in the organization or the content of your paper, then you have embarked upon the final draft without being fully prepared. If this is the case, consider this draft as another revision and work out your problems before again attempting to produce the final draft.

There are two more jobs you must do before you begin to prepare the manuscript of your paper. You must write a complete set of notes acknowledging the source of each quotation or paraphrase in the paper, and you must prepare a final version of your bibliography. The next chapter discusses the form and placement of these source citations.

Review Questions

1. At least how many versions of a research paper must you write? Why?
2. What should you do when your sources disagree?
3. Briefly outline the steps in revising a rough draft.

Exercise

Revise three consecutive paragraphs in your rough draft until you are satisfied with the entire sequence. Show every stage of your revision and explain your reasons for making each change.

8

Documenting Your Sources

When writing your first research paper, you may think of documentation as a nuisance, a mere formality, coming as it does after you have completed the most important parts of the research assignment—finding information and writing the paper. Nevertheless, there are good reasons for executing these finishing touches with care.

Sometimes a reader will want to know where to find further information on your topic. At other times, a reader may want to know how authoritative a particular statement is—that is, whether the source's author is an expert in the field or simply a professional writer summarizing expert opinion for the general public. Even the date of publication can be significant. For example, Sigmund Freud spent more than forty years developing the psychoanalytic theory of personality, and over that period he revised some of his early ideas considerably. If you were to quote or refer to a statement by Freud, a well-informed reader might wonder when Freud made that statement. For that reason, you must be careful to find out the year of *first* publication for every source. Do not stop when you learn the year in which it was *printed,* because many books are printed more than once and by more than one publisher.

Most important of all, the documentation gives your readers a general sense of how well you have done your research. The bibliography reveals at a glance the range of your investigation; the footnotes indicate how thoroughly you read the sources.

What to Document

While writing the rough draft of your paper, you noted in the margins the source of every idea and piece of information that came from your note cards. Now that the paper is finished, you can assign each item a number and produce a full set of notes in the format approved by your instructor. The sources you have noted will appear in your bibliography.

Two questions arise at this point.

- Is it necessary to document the source of every piece of information that you found through your reading?
- Do you have to name a source for information that you already knew before you undertook the research?

You may well wonder whether it is necessary to state where you found facts such as these: the Battle of Chickamauga was fought on September 19 and 20, 1863; 78 percent of the earth's atmosphere is composed of nitrogen; or, the capital of Chad is Ndjamena. Moreover, you might already have known this sort of fact when you began your research. Depending on the nature of your research topic, identifying the source of every such item could hopelessly clutter your paper with notes. To prevent this from happening, it is generally agreed that certain kinds of factual information do not require documentation.

THREE CATEGORIES IN WHICH DOCUMENTATION IS NECESSARY

Putting the matter the other way around, we can say that precise documentation is required for any information that falls into one of these three categories:

1. opinions, judgments, theories, and personal explanations
2. "facts" that are open to dispute and virtually all statistics regarding human behavior
3. factual information gathered by a small number of observers, no matter how expert they may be (for example, the results of a recent scientific experiment)

The facts regarding Chickamauga, nitrogen, and Ndjamena, however, come under the heading of "general knowledge"—information that is readily available to anyone having access to a library, even a very small one. To make footnotes and bibliographies less cumbersome, facts that can be regarded as general knowledge do not have to be documented. To be safe, however, you should consult individual instructors for their opinions on this matter.

Opinions, Judgments, Theories, and Personal Explanations. Encyclopedias are filled with facts that are considered general knowledge, but that does not mean that all information found in an encyclopedia can go into your paper without a note. In the following encyclopedia entry, the annotated passages constitute opinions and would therefore require notes if you used them in your paper.

"influenced . . . by her French contemporaries" is an inference; "greatly" indicates a judgment

"refreshing simplicity," "vigorous treatment," and "pleasing color" involve personal observations and judgments

CASSATT, Mary (1845–1926). American figure painter and etcher, b. Pittsburgh. Most of her life was spent in France, where she was greatly influenced by her great French contemporaries, particularly Manet and Degas, whose friendship and esteem she enjoyed. She allied herself with the impressionists early in her career. Motherhood was Cassatt's most frequent subject. Her pictures are notable for their refreshing simplicity, vigorous treatment, and pleasing color. She excelled also as a pastelist and etcher, and her drypoints and color prints are greatly admired. She is well represented in public and private galleries in the United States. Her best known paintings include several versions of *Mother and Child* (Metropolitan Mus.; Mus. of Fine Arts, Boston; Worcester, Mass., Art Museum); *Lady at the Tea-Table* (Metropolitan Mus.); *Modern Women*, a mural painted for the Women's Building at the Chicago Exposition; and a portrait of the artist's mother. See catalog by A. D. Breeskin (1970); biography by J. M. Carson (1966).

"Facts Open to Dispute." This category includes commonly accepted "facts" based largely on inference. When new evidence is discovered, new inferences may have to be made. For example, the significance of a particular fossil bone is definitely a matter of judgment, and the astronomical phenomenon known as a "black hole" is by no means as factual as many popular accounts suggest.

Much of the work done by behavioral scientists consists of collecting statistical information (the average number of children in Chinese-American families, the rate of juvenile crime in Boston, and so on). Although the statistics you encounter in your research may seem to be hard facts, these facts can be disputed, and theories and conclusions based on such facts are continually debated by the experts. Therefore, almost all information in the behavioral sciences must be documented except historical facts about individual persons and events in the field.

Factual Information Gathered by a Small Number of Observers. Information gathered by observation and experimentation is subject to dispute. The results of similar experiments may vary, or different researchers may interpret identical results differently. Accordingly, such information should be documented so your readers know its source.

INFORMATION PREVIOUSLY KNOWN

Now to the second question you may have had: Is it necessary to provide sources for ideas and information which you were aware of before doing your research? If the information falls into one of the three categories just listed, you must take the time to find a source for it. This will show your readers where they can find more information about the point you have made, and assure them that the information comes from an authoritative source. Furthermore, finding a source would protect you from misremembering what you had read or heard much earlier. You should therefore be sure to record every piece of relevant information and its source, even if the information is already familiar to you.

Basic Information Provided by Documentation

Footnotes and bibliographical entries answer four basic questions— who? what? where? when?

footnote
[1]Jeremy Bernstein, _Einstein_ (New York: Vintage, 1973), p. 231.

bibliography
entry
Bernstein, Jeremy. _Einstein_. New York: Vintage, 1973.

Note the differences between these two forms, especially the punctuation and the order of the author's first and last names. A footnote provides a bit more information than a bibliography entry; it states exactly where (for example, "p. 23") a particular idea or piece of information appears within a source.

Although the task of documenting sources should be a simple matter, scholars in various fields have not yet agreed upon a single standard format. Therefore, you must find out from every instructor which form he or she prefers. Most teachers of language and literature follow the guidelines set down by the Modern Language Association, and this book uses that format in its examples. On pages 150–156 you will find other formats used in the natural and social sciences as well as in other disciplines in the humanities.

The Bibliography

You should already have the information required in your bibliography on the three- by five-inch cards that you filled out in the early stages of your research. With your bibliography completed you should have no trouble writing your footnotes or endnotes, which will be based on the bibliography and the notes you have recorded in the margins of your drafts. It is therefore recommended that you prepare a draft of your bibliography before going on to your notes, even though in the final paper the notes will precede the bibliography. Remember that every source referred to in a footnote must appear in your bibliography.

GENERAL GUIDELINES

A list of your sources must appear at the end of your paper. Arrange the items alphabetically according to the authors' last names so that a reader can find a particular author's name quickly. If a source has no known author, as is the case with many newspaper accounts and editorials, enter it alphabetically according to the first word of its title (ignoring *A, An,* or *The*). See the sample bibliography on pages 141–142.

Do not inflate your bibliography by including items that were not direct sources of information for your paper. In general, no item should appear in your bibliography unless at least one footnote in the paper refers to it.

Common Bibliographic Forms

The following examples illustrate the appropriate forms for the nine most common types of printed sources. Bibliographic forms for citing less common printed sources and nonprinted sources begin on p. 138.

BOOK BY A SINGLE AUTHOR

note punctuation   Thomas, Lewis. <u>The Lives of a Cell</u>. New York:
                        Viking, 1974.

BOOK BY TWO AUTHORS

authors' names in the   Bar—Adon, Aaron, and Werner F. Leopold. <u>Child</u>
order in which they   <u>Language</u>. Englewood Cliffs, N.J.:
appear on title page   Prentice—Hall, 1971.
of source

BOOK BY MORE THAN TWO AUTHORS (ALTERNATE FORMS)

including all authors' names is usually preferable; authors are listed in the order given on title page of source

Dugan, James, Robert C. Cowen, Bill Barada, and Richard M. Crum. World Beneath the Sea. Washington, D.C.: National Geographic Society, 1967.

Dugan, James, et al. World Beneath the Sea. Washington, D.C.: National Geographic Society, 1967.

MORE THAN ONE SOURCE WRITTEN BY THE SAME AUTHOR

line of ten hyphens is used in place of author's name for all entries after the first, even for titles that have one or more co-authors; several titles by a single author or the same co-authors are usually arranged by publication date, although alphabetical order by title is sometimes used; co-authored books follow singly authored books alphabetically by co-author

Thomas, Lewis. The Lives of a Cell. New York: Viking, 1974.

——————. The Medusa and the Snail. New York: Viking, 1979.

Chomsky, Noam. Syntactic Structures. The Hague: Mouton, 1957.

——————, and Morris Halle. The Sound Pattern of English. New York: Harper & Row, 1968.

——————, and George A. Miller. Analyse Formelle Des Langues Naturelles. No. 8 of Mathematiques et Sciences De L'homme. The Hague: Mouton, 1971.

ESSAY APPEARING IN A BOOK:

"Eds." stands for "editors," the compilers of the book's essays or other writings; pages on which full essay appears are shown, even if only a page or two are used as sources

Frake, Charles O. "How to Ask for a Drink in Subanum." In Directions in Sociolinguistics. Eds. John J. Gumperz and D. Hymes. New York: Holt, Rinehart and Winston, 1972, pp. 127–32.

ARTICLE IN AN ANNUAL, SEMIANNUAL, OR QUARTERLY PERIODICAL

when author's name is not given, source is listed by title; if the organization that published the periodical is significant, that information is included; note that "p." and "pp." are not used when volume number is given; pages on which the full article appears are shown

Moore, John B. "The Role of Gulliver." Modern
    Philological Quarterly, 25 (1928),
    169–80.

"Do Cities Change the Weather?" Mosaic,
    (Washington, D.C.: National Science
    Foundation), 5 (Summer 1974), 29–34.

ARTICLE IN A MONTHLY PERIODICAL

date is enclosed in parentheses only when volume number is given; "p." and "pp." are used only when the volume number is not given (you have the option to show the volume number or not); "pp. 12–13, 113" shows that article was completed at end of magazine

Premack, Ann James, and David Premack.
    "Teaching Language to an Ape."
    Scientific American, 227 (Oct. 1972),
    92–99.

Sahgal, Pavan. "Idiot Geniuses." Science
    Digest, May 1981, pp. 12–13, 113.

ARTICLE IN A WEEKLY PERIODICAL

issue is identified by date, month, and year

Dorschner, John. "Look Out! Here Comes the
    Sahara!" Tropic, 29 Dec. 1974, pp.
    34–45.
"Women's Bank: A Modest Profit." Newsweek, 20
    April 1981, p. 16.

ARTICLE IN A NEWSPAPER

when only writer's initials are known, they follow normal order (not "K., J."); note quotation marks within quotation marks in the third example; section number or letter, if there is one, is included; when the paper's title does not include the name of the city, that information is shown in parentheses (the *Daily Worker* was a *national* newspaper)

Roughton, Roger. "Barber's Bust with Loaf on Head." Daily Worker, 8 April 1936, p. 7.

J. K. "Explodes an Illusion." Daily Worker, 30 Dec. 1936, pp. 7–8.

"Presidential Panel Holds Hearings on 'Right to Die.' " New York Times, 12 April 1981, Sec. 1, p. 24.

"Rebirth of a City." News–Times (Danbury, Conn.), 6 Sept. 1977, p. 2.

Some Less Common Bibliographic Forms

BOOK THAT IS A VOLUME IN A SERIES

a volume will often have its own title; if that tile is prominent in its own right, it is cited first; if the volume is known chiefly as part of a larger work, the larger work's title is cited with the volume's number; in such cases volume title is often omitted

Nevins, Allan. The Organized War, 1863–64. Vol. III of The War for the Union. New York: Scribner's, 1971.
Wellek, René. A History of Modern Criticism: 1750–1950. Vol. 2. New Haven: Yale University Press, 1955.

OR

Wellek, René. A History of Modern Criticism: 1750–1950. Vol. 2: The Romantic Age. New Haven: Yale University Press, 1955.

BOOK PUBLISHED IN SEVERAL VOLUMES

bibliographic entry indicates that all three volumes have been used

Dickinson, Emily. The Poems of Emily Dickinson. Ed. Thomas H. Johnson. 3 vols. Cambridge, Mass.: The Belknap Press, Harvard University Press, 1955.

FOREWORD, PREFACE, OR AFTERWORD TO A BOOK

reference here is to Edel's rather than Wilson's writing; had Wilson's text also been cited, book would be entered twice, once under each author's name

Edel, Leon. Foreword. The Thirties. By Edmund Wilson, New York: Farrar, Straus & Giroux, 1980.

EDITOR'S COMMENTS IN A BOOK

Gardner rather than Carroll is cited

Gardner, Martin, ed. The Annotated Alice. Alice's Adventures in Wonderland and Through the Looking Glass. By Lewis Carroll (Charles Dodgson). New York: Clarkson Potter, 1960.

REVIEW OF ANOTHER WORK

Chomsky rather than Skinner is cited

Chomsky, Noam. "Review of B.F. Skinner's Verbal Behavior." Language, 35 (1959), 26–58.

PUBLICATION OF A CORPORATION OR A GOVERNMENT AGENCY

both could also be entered by title; choice is compiler's

Federal Council for Science and Technology. First Annual Report of Ad Hoc Committee on Geodynamics. USIGP-F476, Washington, 1976.

Phillips Petroleum. 66 Ways to Save Energy. Bartlesville, Okla., 1978.

REVISED OR ENLARGED EDITION

editions other than first must be identified

Chomsky, Noam. Language and Mind. Enl. ed. New York: Harcourt Brace Jovanovich, 1972.

REPRINTED EDITION

note distinction between reprint and revised edition; revision means that changes were made, and date given is that of the changes; reprint leaves everything as in the original; important date is that of the first writing

Boys, C. V. <u>Soap Bubbles and the Forces Which Mould Them</u>. 1916; rpt. New York: Doubleday, 1959.

ARTICLE IN AN ENCYCLOPEDIA OR SIMILAR REFERENCE WORK

although article's title is "Isaac Newton," it is entered under "Newton," under which a reader would look it up; second example shows form for signed article

"Newton, Isaac." <u>The New Columbia Encyclopedia</u>, 1975.

Kaufmann, Walter. "Nietzsche, Friedrich." <u>Encyclopaedia Britannica</u>, 1969.

UNSIGNED PAMPHLET

both writer and publisher unknown

<u>Push for Pot</u>. Ann Arbor, n. pub., 1969.

OFFICIAL TESTIMONY

note absence of underlining or quotation marks

Altshuller, Aubrey P. Testimony before the Subcommittee on the Environment and the Atmosphere. Committee on Science and Technology, House of Representatives, 22 May, 1975.

LECTURE

Thomas, Lewis. "Notes of a Biology Watcher." Lecture at the Princeton Club of New York, 21 Feb. 1978.

TELEVISION PROGRAM

Marshall was
program's narrator

"Gorilla." <u>National Geographic Society</u>. Narr.
E. G. Marshall, WNET–PBS, 15 April 1981.

FILM

can be entered either
by title or director,
depending on how
used as a source:
when studying
director's work, name
is given first; when
studying film itself
(as art form or as
adaptation of a novel)
title is used

<u>Clockwork Orange, A</u>. Dir. Stanley Kubrick.
Based on <u>Clockwork Orange</u> by Anthony
Burgess. 1971.
Kubrick, Stanley, dir. <u>2001: A Space Odyssey</u>.
1969.

RECORDING

again purpose
dictates order in
which information is
presented: when
topic is music,
second form is used;
when artist is topic,
his/her name is
entered; when artist
or author is identified
by nickname or
pseudonym, supply
the true name in
parenthesis

Leadbelly (Huddie Ledbetter). <u>Rock Island
Line</u>. Notes by Frederic Ramsey, Jr.
Folkways, FA 2014.
"Black Girl." <u>Rock Island Line</u>. Sung by
Leadbelly (Huddie Ledbetter). Folkways,
FA 2014.

SAMPLE LIST OF SOURCES

compiler has chosen
to list Chomsky
material
alphabetically by
title; co-authored
works follow singly
authored works

Chomsky, Noam. <u>Language and Mind</u>. Rev. ed. New
York: Harcourt Brace Jovanovich, 1972.
——————. "Review of B. F. Skinner's
<u>Verbal Behavior</u>." <u>Language</u>, 35 (1959), 26–
58.
——————. <u>Syntactic Structures</u>. The Hague:
Mouton, 1957.

----------, and Morris Halle. The Sound
Pattern of English. New York: Harper &
Row, 1968.

Clockwork Orange, A. Directed by Stanley
Kubrick. Based on Clockwork Orange by
Anthony Burgess. 1971.

"Do Cities Change the Weather?" Mosaic
(Washington, D.C.: National Science
Foundation), 5(Summer 1974), 29-34.

J. K. "Explodes an Illusion." Daily Worker, 30
Dec. 1936, pp. 7-8.

Kaufmann, Walter. "Nietzsche, Friedrich."
Encyclopaedia Britannica, 1969.

Footnotes and Endnotes

The word *footnote* comes from its traditional position at the foot of a page. Even experienced typists, however, have trouble gauging how much room to leave for notes at the bottom of a page while the page is being typed, and many instructors prefer students to list their footnotes separately from the text, at the end of the paper, just before the bibliography. These are then called *endnotes*. Check with each instructor for whom you are doing research to see whether endnotes are acceptable.

The format for notes differs only slightly from that for bibliography entries. The main difference is that a note identifies the page in a source on which you found a particular idea or piece of information. A note is numbered to correspond with an idea that is given that same number in the text of your paper (see p. 149). In the note, the number is indented five spaces and raised half a space. You then skip a space and proceed to give the necessary information. The basic mark of punctuation in a note is the *comma* instead of the *period*.

Basic Forms for Endnotes

BOOK BY A SINGLE AUTHOR

note punctuation and spacing as well as order of the author's first and last names

[1] Lewis Thomas, The Lives of a Cell (New York: Viking, 1974), p.88.

BOOK BY TWO AUTHORS

[2] Aaron Bar-Adon and Werner F. Leopold, Child Language (Englewood Cliffs, N.J.: Prentice-Hall, 1971), pp. 123-24.

BOOK BY MORE THAN TWO AUTHORS

unlike a bibliographic entry, use of "et al." is recommended; abbreviation of publisher is acceptable in note

[3] James Dugan, et al., World Beneath the Sea (Washington, D.C.: Nat. Geog. Soc., 1967), pp. 78-79.

ESSAY APPEARING IN A BOOK

[4] Charles O. Frake, "How to Ask for a Drink in Subanum," in Directions in Sociolinguistics, eds. John J. Gumperz and D. Hymes (New York: Holt, Rinehart and Winston, 1972), p. 130.

ARTICLE IN AN ANNUAL, SEMIANNUAL, OR QUARTERLY PERIODICAL

titles of periodicals are abbreviated if correct form (used in bibliographies and periodical Indexes) is known

[5] John B. Moore, "The Role of Gulliver," MPQ, 25 (1928), 170.

quotation marks and exclamation points in titles are not followed by commas; note abbreviation of publisher

[6] "Do Cities Change the Weather?" Mosaic (Washington: Nat. Sci. Fdn.), 5 (Summer 1974), 32-33.

ARTICLE IN A MONTHLY PERIODICAL

[7] Pavan Sahgal, "Idiot Geniuses," Sci. Dig., May 1981, p. 12.

ARTICLE IN A WEEKLY PERIODICAL

no comma after the
exclamation point in
first title

[8] John Dorschner, "Look Out! Here Comes the Sahara!" _Tropic_, 29 Dec., 1974, pp. 43–44.
[9] "Women's Bank: A Modest Profit," _Newsweek_, 20 Apr., 1981, p. 16.

ARTICLE IN A NEWSPAPER

[10] Roger Roughton, "Barber's Bust with Loaf on Head," _Daily Worker_, 8 April, 1936, p. 7.
[11] "Rebirth of a City," _News–Times_ (Danbury, Conn.), 6 Sept., 1977, p. 2.

Less Common Note Forms

BOOK THAT IS A VOLUME IN A SERIES

[12] Allan Nevins, _The Organized War, 1863–64_, vol. III of _The War for the Union_ (New York: Scribner's, 1971), pp.120–21.

BOOK PUBLISHED IN SEVERAL VOLUMES

note the changed
position of volume
number from
bibliography

[13] Emily Dickinson, _The Poems of Emily Dickinson_, ed. Thomas H. Johnson (Cambridge, Mass.: The Belknap Press, Harvard University Press, 1955), II, 157.

FOREWORD, PREFACE, OR AFTERWORD TO A BOOK

[14] Leon Edel, Foreword, _The Thirties_, by Edmund Wilson (New York: Farrar, Straus & Giroux, 1980), pp. 2–3.

EDITOR'S COMMENTS IN A BOOK

some books use
roman numerals as
page numbers for
introductory remarks

[15] Martin Gardner, ed., The Annotated
Alice, Alice's Adventures in Wonderland
and Through the Looking Glass, by Lewis Carroll
(New York: Clarkson Potter, 1960), pp. iv–v.

REVIEW OF ANOTHER WORK

[16] Noam Chomsky, "Review of B. F. Skinner's
Verbal Behavior," Language, 35 (1959), 29–30.

PUBLICATION OF A CORPORATION OR A
GOVERNMENT AGENCY

[17] Federal Council for Science and
Technology, First Annual Report of Ad Hoc
Committee on Geodynamics (USIGP–F476,
Washington, 1976), p. 342.
   [18] Phillips Petroleum, 66 Ways to Save
Energy (Bartlesville, Okla., 1978), p. 5.

REVISED OR ENLARGED EDITION

[19] Noam Chomsky, Language and Mind, enl.
ed. (New York: Harcourt Brace Jovanovich,
1972), pp. 199–200.

REPRINTED EDITION

[20] C. V. Boys, Soap Bubbles and the Forces
Which Mould Them (1916; rpt. New York:
Doubleday, 1959), p. 42.

ARTICLE IN AN ENCYCLOPEDIA OR SIMILAR
REFERENCE WORK

order of words in title
of article is the same
as in bibliography

[21] "Newton, Isaac," The New Columbia
Encyclopedia (1975).

page numbers are
not given because
the reader can
readily locate the
article by title
alphabetically; if
article continues for
several pages,
appropriate page
number is given

22 Walter Kaufmann, "Nietzsche,
Friedrich," Encyclopaedia Britannica (1969).

UNSIGNED PAMPHLET

pages were not
numbered; that
information cannot
be given

23 Push for Pot (Ann Arbor: n. pub., 1969).

OFFICIAL TESTIMONY

some government
publications do not
use page numbers;
that information
cannot be given

24 Aubrey P. Altshuller, Testimony before
the Subcommittee on the Environment and the
Atmosphere, Committee on Science and
Technology, House of Representatives, 22 May,
1975.

LECTURE

25 Lewis Thomas, "Notes of a Biology
Watcher," lecture at the Princeton Club of New
York, 21 Feb. 1978.

TELEVISION PROGRAM

26"Gorilla," National Geographic Society,
narr. E. G. Marshall, WNET–PBS, 15 April 1981.

FILM

27 A Clockwork Orange, dir. Stanley
Kubrick, based on Clockwork Orange, by Anthony
Burgess, 1971.
28 Stanley Kubrick, dir., 2001: A Space
Odyssey, 1969.

RECORDING

²⁹ Leadbelly (Huddie Ledbetter), <u>Rock Island Line</u>, with notes by Frederic Ramsey, Jr., Folkways, FA 2014.

³⁰ "Black Girl," Rock Island Line, sung by Leadbelly (Huddie Ledbetter), Folkways, FA 2014.

Footnote Format

True footnotes, those placed at the bottoms of pages rather than collected at the end of the paper, contain the same information in the same order as endnotes. The only difference is that endnotes are double-spaced within the notes as well as between notes, as in the sample paper on Jefferson Davis. Footnotes are usually single-spaced within the notes but double-spaced between notes. See the sample paper on Emily Dickinson.

THE SHORT FORM FOR NOTES

When more than one of your notes refers to the same source, only the first of these notes must provide all the bibliographic information about the source. Other references to that source need only include the author's name or the source's title; for example:

full form

¹ Jeremy Bernstein, <u>Einstein</u> (New York: Vintage, 1973), p. 19.

short form

⁴ Bernstein, pp. 99–101.

short form if author is mentioned in paper's text

⁷ <u>Einstein</u>, p. 146.

The short form must not, however, be so short as to confuse a reader. If two authors among your sources have the same last name, or if two or more sources were written by the same person, you must expand the short form enough to avoid confusion.

short forms for two sources written by same person

⁷ Thomas, <u>Lives of a Cell</u>, p. 47.

⁸ Thomas, <u>Medusa and the Snail</u>, pp. 134–35.

¹¹ Chomsky, <u>Language and Mind</u>, p. 231.

¹² Chomsky and Halle, p. 71–72.

long titles can be
shortened to a few
distinctive words as
long as there is no
chance for confusion

[9] Federal Council for Science and
Technology <u>First Annual Report of Ad Hoc
Committee on Geodynamics</u>, (USIGP–F476,
Washington, 1976), p. 342.
. . . . .

[13] <u>Report on Geodynamics</u>, pp. 222–23.
. . . . .

[14] Noam Chomsky, "Review of B. F. Skinner's
<u>Verbal Behavior</u>," <u>Language</u>, 35 (1959), 29–30.
. . . . .

[18] Chomsky, "Review of Skinner," p. 56.

In your previous readings, you may have seen the abbreviation *ibid.* ("in the same place"), which means that the note refers to the same source as the one in the note just ahead of it. This was once the standard short form for a series of notes that all referred to the same source, but it is no longer standardly used because it can occasionally be confusing. If you are careful with the short form shown here, there should be no confusion.

NOTES THAT REFER TO LITERARY WORKS

If your paper deals with specific works of literature, you may find yourself frequently quoting or referring to passages in these works. In that case, you would need to identify the page numbers of a novel or short story, or the lines of a long poem or a play. To insert a note each time you did this would constantly interrupt your readers who might well look up each note to see what you had to say. To save your readers this trouble, place the necessary information inside parentheses within the text of your papers.

note that the
parenthetical
information appears
before the period at
the end of the
sentence

Shakespeare deftly shifts images in
Othello's speech over the sleeping Desdemona,
from lightness of color (Desdemona as opposed
to Othello) to light as a symbol of life (V,
ii, 3–13).

It would seem that Ahab has forever
rejected God as he commences his final
soliloquy with, "I turn my body from the
sun . . ." (p. 468).

Before using notes such as these, you must provide one regular note that identifies the edition of the work you are using.

in the first note, it must be stated that all subsequent references to the work refer to that edition

[1] Shakespeare, Othello, in The Complete Works of Shakespeare, rev. Hardin Craig and David Bevington, 2nd ed. (Glenview, Ill: Scott, Foresman, 1973), pp. 947–79. All further references will be to this edition.

PLACING NOTE NUMBERS IN THE TEXT

All notes are to be numbered consecutively through the paper. If you come to the end of your paper and discover that you left a note number out, you must insert the correct number and then change all succeeding numbers to maintain the proper sequence.

The number is typed a half space above the line, immediately after the sentence which contains the information you referred to. That is, do not leave any space between the final mark of punctuation and the number.

. . . their final year in Warsaw. [9]
. . . said, "War is Hell!" [10]

An exception occurs when you refer, in one of your paragraphs, to several pieces of information that you found on the same page (or several consecutive pages) of a source. In such a case, to avoid cluttering your text with note numbers, you can put just one number at the end of the paragraph. This situation happens most often when you have summarized part or all of a source, as in the example on page 100.

Documentation of Illustrative Materials

A final matter regarding documentation concerns the layout and labeling of graphs, tables, and other illustrative materials.

Tables are referred to as "tables," but graphs, pictures, diagrams, and other kinds of illustration are all referred to as "figures." Each kind of item is numbered consecutively throughout the paper with arabic numerals (Table 1, Table 2; Figure 1, Figure 2, Figure 3).

TABLE 1

U.S.-JAPAN MERCHANDISE TRADE: 1975-1978

Year	U.S. domestic exports to Japan	U.S. general imports from Japan
1975	$ 9,421,000,000	$11,268,000,000
1976	10,027,000,000	15,504,000,000
1977	10,422,000,000	18,550,000,000
1978	12,689,000,000	24,458,000,000

Source: U.S. Bureau of the Census, Statistical Abstract of the United
   States: 1979. (Washington, D.C.: GPO, 1979), p. 920.

FIGURE 1

figure shows U.S.-JAPAN MERCHANDISE TRADE: 1975-1978
same information as
preceding table;
captions below
the figure are
sometimes used
instead of
titles above

Billions
of
dollars

Source: U.S. Bureau of the Census,
   Statistical Abstract of the United
   States: 1979. (Washington, D.C.:
   GPO, 1979). p. 920.

Other Forms of Documentation

For papers written about subjects in the behavioral and natural sciences, you may be required to use considerably different forms of documentation from that used for papers submitted in humanities courses.
The only similarity between the various systems of documentation is
that in all cases you need to identify, in some fashion, the *author* and
the *date of publication*.

Two general approaches serve as models for the specific formats employed by the various disciplines: the *author/year system*, and the *numbered system*. These two systems share one important feature—they do not use either footnotes or endnotes. The documentary information is presented just once, in the list of references. Very brief notes referring readers to items on the list of references are placed within the text itself, inside parentheses.

Although each discipline has its own generally accepted format, within a single field you may find instructors who require slight variations. These instructors will usually announce their preferences, but if an instructor says nothing in class about the form to be used for a paper, be sure to inquire before typing the paper for submission.

THE AUTHOR/YEAR SYSTEM

When using this system, you do not place note numbers in the text, nor do you prepare a list of endnotes. You merely refer briefly to items on your bibliography within parentheses. If you mention the author's name at the time you refer to information in the source, you enter the date of publication within parentheses just after the author's name. If you do not mention the author when referring to the source, then put both the author's name and the date of publication within parentheses at the end of the sentence referring to the source.

when source has several authors, "et al." may be used

Jones (1972) states that whenever . . .

Further testing (Jakes and Acker, 1975) revealed . . .

Several studies (Morgan, 1974; Edwards, 1975; Borgen, 1977) have shown that . . .

A recent survey (Bloss, et al., 1978) shows . . .

List of references. Arrange the sources in alphabetical order. Two or more items written by the same person appear in chronological order. When two or more items written by the same person have been published during the same year, place small letters after the years to distinguish them in both the body of the paper and the list of references.

note that article and chapter titles are not set off with quotation marks

Erikson, E. H. (1950a). <u>Childhood and Society</u>. New York: Norton.
————. (1950b). Growth Crises of the Healthy Personality. In <u>Identity and the</u>

titles are often not
capitalized after the
first word; colon
separates volume
(often underlined)
from pages

<u>Life Cycle</u>. New York: International
Universities Press.
——————. (1956). The Problem of Ego
Identity. <u>J. Amer. Psychoanal. Assn.</u>,
<u>4</u>: 56–121.
——————. (1963). Youth: Fidelity and
Diversity. In E. H. Erikson (Ed.),
<u>The Challenge of Youth</u>. New York:
Doubleday.
——————(Ed.). (1968). <u>Identity: Youth
and Crisis</u>. New York: Norton.

For books, some disciplines ask you to show the total number of
pages. For periodical articles, always show the pages on which the full
article appears. Bibliographic formats differ from one discipline to another. Examples for a range of disciplines follow the description of the
numbered system.

THE NUMBERED SYSTEM

Each entry in the list of references is assigned a number, and each
note in the text consists of just that number (or the author's name and
the number), unless additional information seems necessary. As with
the author/year system, this information is enclosed in parentheses in
the text.

names can be left out
when several
sources are
mentioned

Widlow (4) found that . . .

Breitenstein and Forester (7) showed that . . .

Morgan (11) and Stanley (6) both argued
that . . .

A recent experiment (Moss, 3) determined that . . .

Recent evidence (8,13,19) seems to indicate . . .

When writing scientific papers, you do not usually refer to specific
pages, and page numbers in the text of your paper are therefore un-
necessary. The exception to this rule occurs in those rare instances
when you quote your source. In such cases, the page number appears
within the parentheses along with the source number.

direct quotation

As Elsasser (5, p. 17) stated, "The outcome . . ."

List of References. Some disciplines require you to list your sources in the order in which you refer to them in your paper; others require alphabetical listings. If you have a choice, list your sources in the order in which you refer to them in your paper.

Forms for Lists of References in Disciplines Outside the Humanities

Be sure to note the differences in the following matters:

- the placing of the date of publication
- the use of underlining and quotation marks for titles
- the use of abbreviations for periodical titles

SCIENCES

Biology uses the numbered system with references in alphabetical order.

most publications do not capitalize first letters of words after the first in titles unless they are proper nouns; when article appears on just one page, page number is repeated as in second note; date follows all other information

1. Bernal, J. D., and I. Frankuchen. X–ray and crystallographic studies of plant virus preparations. J. Gen. Physio. 25:111–165; 1941.
2. Crick, F. H. C. Is α–keratin a coiled coil? Nature. 170:882–882; 1952.
3. Judson, H. F. The eighth day of creation. Simon & Schuster, New York; 1979.

Botany and *Zoology* use the author/year system with references in alphabetical order.

first letters of words after the first in titles are not capitalized, except for proper nouns; volume numbers are underlined

Hairston, N. G., F. E. Smith, and L. B. Slobodkin. 1960. Community, structure, population, control, and competition. American Naturalist 94: 421–425.

Muller, W. H. 1974. Botany: a functional approach. Macmillan, New York. 601 p.

Chemistry uses the numbered system with references in the order in which they are cited in the paper.

note omission of
titles for periodical
articles and use of
quotation marks for
book titles

(1) T. Raptolinsky, "Chemists and the New
    Technology," Mills Ltd., Manchester,
    1976, pp. 102–109.

(2) R. Johnstone, J. Am. Chem. Soc., 89,
    405–412 (1978).

(3) L. Pauling, R. B. Corey, and H. R. Branson,
    Proc. N. A. S., 37, 205–211 (1951).

Engineering uses numbered system with references in the order in which they are cited in the paper.

1. Keenan, J. H., and Keyes, F. G.
   Thermodynamic Properties of Steam, Wiley,
   New York, 1936.

2. Cook, E. G. "Stress Patterns in Danbury
   Bridge," ACBL 42, August 1979.

Geology uses the author/year system and alphabetical order.

follows same format
as botany and
zoology, except that
order of the publisher
and city is reversed

Purrett, L. A. 1972. Before Pangaea—what?
    Science News 102: 220–222.
Sullivan, W. 1974. Continents in motion. New
    York, McGraw-Hill. 399 p.

Mathematics uses the numbered system and alphabetical order.

note that all titles are
underlined

1. Petr Beckmann, A History of Pi, New York,
   St. Martin's, 1976.

2. Paul Bennacerraf, God, the Devil, and
   Goedel, Monist 51 (1967), 9.

3. J. R. Lucas, Minds, Machines, and
   Goedel, in Minds and Machines, ed. A. R.
   Anderson, Englewood Cliffs, N.J.,
   Prentice-Hall, 1964.

Physics uses the numbered system with references in the order in which they are cited.

page numbers for
books tell which
pages are relevant to
paper

[1]A. Baker, Modern Physics and Anti-physics
   (Addison-Wesley, Reading, Mass., 1970),
   pp. 45–49, 102–10.

titles of articles are not given; titles of periodicals are not underlined

[2]J. M. Jauch, <u>Are Quanta Real? A Galilean Dialogue</u> (Indiana University Press, Bloomington, 1973), pp. 72–77.

[3]D. R. Hofstadter, Physical Review B, <u>14</u>, no. 6, 45–64 (1976).

SOCIAL SCIENCES

Economics uses the author/year system and alphabetical order.

note that last item, although numbered like a periodical, is a pamphlet or small book and no page numbers are given

R. Easterlin, "Does Money Buy Happiness?" <u>The Public Interest</u>, Winter 1973, 30, 1–17.

E. E. Lawler II, <u>Pay and Organizational Effectiveness: A Psychological View</u>, New York, 1971.

United States Department of Commerce, <u>Survey of Current Business</u>, July 1979, 59, no. 7.

Education uses either the humanities format or the author/year system and alphabetical order.

preferred form

Bruner, Jerome S., "The Growth of Mind," <u>Amer. Psychol.</u> 20: 1007–17; Oct. 1977.

Jones, Richard M., <u>Fantasy and Feeling in Education</u>. New York: New York University Press, 1968. 276 p.

History usually follows the humanities format.

Political Science usually follows the humanities format.

Psychology commonly uses the author/year system, but some journals use the numbered system. Both systems follow alphabetical order. Ask your instructor which to use.

preferred form

Blos, P. (1962), <u>On Adolescence</u>. New York: Free Press.

Erikson, E. H. (1956), The Problem of Ego Identity. <u>J. Amer. Psychoanal. Assn.</u>, 4: 56–121.

```
                  Mahler, M. S., Pine, F., and Bergman, A.
                     (1975), The Psychological Birth of the
                     Human Infant. New York: Basic Books.
```

Sociology uses the author/year system and alphabetical order. Book titles are not always underlined and article titles are not always capitalized after the first word or enclosed in quotation marks. Find out your instructor's preferences.

preferred form
```
                  Gumperz, John J. (1971) Language in Social
                     Groups. Stanford, Calif.: Stanford
                     University Press.
                  Maranda, Elli (1971) "Theory and Practice of
                     Riddle Analysis." Jour. Amer. Folklore 84
                     (July): 51-61.
```

Review Questions

1. Why do research papers include both notes and a bibliography?
2. Explain why you would or would not document each of these pieces of information in a research paper.

   - the name of Robert E. Lee's father
   - the latest census data about the income and size of the average family in the United States
   - T. S. Eliot's interpretation of the river in *Huckleberry Finn*
   - Dr. Elisabeth Kübler-Ross's study of dying patients
   - William Faulkner's date of birth
   - the latest research about the effects of caffeine

3. How do the forms for a note and a bibliography entry about a book differ?
4. How do the forms for a note and a bibliography entry about a periodical article differ?
5. How do footnotes and endnotes differ?

Exercise

For each of the following items of bibliographic information, write:

- a standard footnote or endnote
- a footnote or endnote using the short form, as it would be written for second or later references to the same source (the page numbers for these later references appear at the end of each description in parentheses)
- a bibliography, listing all the sources in the correct order and using the standard form for each entry

If you need help getting started, the first five of the following items appear in the bibliography for the Dickinson paper in Chapter 9.

1. Your research led you to a book titled Emily Dickinson: A Collection of Critical Essays, in which you found an essay called Emily Dickinson and the Limits of Judgment. The book was edited by Richard B. Sewall, and the essay was the work of Yvor Winters. The essay began on page 38 and ended on page 56; you quoted a comment from page 42. The book was published in 1963 by Prentice-Hall, located in Englewood Cliffs, New Jersey. (Second reference was to page 53.)

2. Your research uncovered an essay, Father and Daughter: Edward and Emily Dickinson, which was published in a journal, American Literature, in January 1960. This was volume 40, and the essay covered pages 510 to 523. The idea which you paraphrased ran from page 519 to page 520. The writer was Owen Thomas. (Second reference was to page 515.)

3. When quoting Emily Dickinson's poetry, you used a collection called The Complete Poems of Emily Dickinson, which was published in 1960 by Little, Brown and Company, located in Boston, Massachusetts. The person who edited the poems was Thomas H. Johnson. The poem you quoted appeared on page 119. (Second quotation came from page 202.)

4. When quoting the poet's letters, you used a three-volume collection called The Letters of Emily Dickinson, which was published in Cambridge, Massachusetts, by the Harvard University Press in 1958. The editors were Thomas H. Johnson and Theodora Ward. The letter you quoted appeared on page 27 of the third volume. (Second reference was to a letter on page 32 of the second volume.)

5. You read a book written by the critic Paul J. Ferlazzo in 1976. The book was titled Emily Dickinson and was published by Twayne Publishers, which is located in Boston, Massachusetts. Your paper referred to a comment on page 98. (Second reference was to page 198.)

6. You read a tribute to the poet, called The First Lady of Mt. Holyoke, which appeared in the South Hadley (Massachusetts) Gazette on December 10, 1980. This unsigned essay appeared on the second and third pages of the second section of the newspaper, and the words you quoted came from the second column on the second page. (Second reference was to the second column, page three.)

7. You also wrote a letter to a professor at Mt. Holyoke College, Joanna Caldwell, who is an authority on the poet and her works. You quoted a remark from her reply to you, which was written on November 4, 1980. The remark appeared on the fourth page of her letter. (Second reference was to page 3.)

8. You read an article in the magazine Psychology Today, written by John Forsyte, Joanna Caldwell, and Edgar Polishook. The article, titled Emily Dickinson: Inhibited Genius?, appeared in the July 1979 issue on pages 68 to 80; you quoted a comment on page 72. (Second reference was a paraphrase of two paragraphs extending from page 74 to page 75.)

9. You read a review of Ferlazzo's book (see item 5), written by Joanna Caldwell, which was published in PMLA, volume 65, pages 343 to 345. This issue was published in May 1980, and your quotation came from page 343. (Second reference was to page 344.)

9

Preparing the Final Manuscript

As you no doubt already know, appearances count. After investing so much time and energy in the research assignment, you would be foolish to hand in a paper containing numerous typographical errors, insertions, and corrections. A messy manuscript could easily lead your reader to think you had done the whole job in haste. Be sure, therefore, to leave enough time for preparing a clean, attractively designed manuscript.

First and foremost, type the paper at all costs. Most instructors will insist that you type research papers, but even if you find one who accepts handwritten papers, you would be wise to get the paper typed, exceptionally neat and easy-to-read handwriting notwithstanding.

Follow precisely whatever format your instructor specifies. If none is recommended, however, the advice given here will help you put your best foot forward.

The Mechanics of Manuscript Preparation

MATERIALS

1. Use 8½-by-11 inch white paper, 20-pound bond.
2. Do not use erasable paper—it smudges easily. Do not use onion-skin paper, either, except for your own carbon copy if you choose to make one.

3. Type on just one side of each page.

4. Use a new ribbon, black only.

SPACING AND MARGINS

1. In general, leave a one-inch margin at the top and bottom of each page and on the left-hand side. Of course, you cannot know where lines will end on the right-hand side, but you should try to leave a one-inch margin there, as well. Break up long words with hyphens before they extend into the margin.
   Exception: The top of the first page looks a bit different. Type the title two inches from the top; then double-space twice before the first line of your text.

2. Double-space lines throughout the paper, including the endnote and bibliography pages.
   Exceptions: 1. Footnotes at the bottoms of the pages are single-spaced with two spaces between notes. 2. Long quotations indented from the margin may be single-spaced.

3. Indent each paragraph five spaces. Long quotations—more than four lines long—should be indented ten spaces and single-spaced, unless your instructor says to double-space. When indenting a long quotation, do not enclose the quotation in quotation marks. (See page 168ff.)

PAGE NUMBERING

Starting with the second page, number each page consecutively in the upper right-hand corner. The bibliography and endnote pages (if you follow endnote style) do not usually have numbers. It is a good idea to type your name below each page number and on the unnumbered pages to prevent confusion if your paper should become mixed up with someone else's.

TITLE PAGE

The following information appears on the title page: the title, your name, your instructor's name, the course and section numbers, and the date on which the paper is submitted. (see pages 162 and 179)

BINDING

In order to keep the pages of your paper together, use a large paperclip or a lightweight, clear plastic folder.

CORRECTIONS

Proofread the final draft with extreme care. If the paper contains a few errors, these may be corrected neatly *in ink*. Make your changes above the lines in which they occur. Do not use the margins for this purpose. Insert a word or phrase neatly above a caret, as in this sentence.

insertion

```
         Most historians today conclude that
         Jefferson Davis, despite his personal
                    probably
         shortcomings, was the most capable
                        ^
         president the South could have chosen.
```

Two Sample Research Papers

Here are two research papers written by students in their first year of college. The papers were selected as samples not only because they demonstrate competence in the research techniques described in this book, but also because the two students were writing for different academic disciplines and therefore used slightly different approaches to their projects.

Jefferson Davis as President: A Confederate Asset

Submitted by George C. Pitman, III
to Professor David Mason

History 121 United States History
Section 7C
November 10, 1981

OUTLINE
Jefferson Davis as President: A Confederate Asset

Introductory paragraph, including the thesis statement
I. Extreme views of Davis's leadership
    A. Negative (Pollard)
        1. Responsibility for loss of the war
            a. Squandering of South's resources
            b. An "imbecile and barren" administration
            c. Personal vanity
        2. Pollard's bias
            a. Personal dislike of Davis
            b. Need for a scapegoat (Patrick)
    B. Positive (Strode)
        1. Davis's strengths
            a. Unselfishness and integrity
            b. Minor nature of his flaws
            c. Refusal to play politics at expense of civil
               liberties
        2. Superiority to Lincoln in regard to civil
           liberties
            a. Implied comparison
            b. Direct comparison (Dodd)
        3. Nobility of Davis in a doomed cause
II. Moderate views of Davis's leadership
    A. One view (Nevins)
        1. Davis's failings
            a. Obsession with details and military matters
            b. "inability to labor amicably" with other
               leaders

      2. Davis's strengths
         a. "Vision" of South's potential greatness
         b. "Unshakable integrity"
         c. Experience in government
         d. Personal dignity
      3. Support for Nevins's view (Randall and Donald)
         a. Weaknesses in administrative and military
            areas
         b. Accomplishments in light of problems faced
   B. Another view (Catton)
      1. Odds against Davis and the South
         a. North's enormous advantages
         b. Dissension within the South (Dodd, too)
      2. A tragic view of Davis
III. Analysis of two major charges against Davis
   A. Reputed weakness as a military leader (Barney)
      1. The charge of "meddling"
         a. The tendency to make scapegoats of losing
            captains (Patrick)
         b. Comparison to Lincoln, another "meddler"
      2. Both sides' ignorance of modern warfare
         a. The nature of war at that time
         b. North's discovery of "war of attrition"
         c. Defense of Davis in this light
   B. Supposed weakness as political leader (Rabun)
      1. Refusal to surrender to special interests
      2. Bitter quarrel between Davis and Stephens
         a. Davis's loyalty to South as a whole
         b. Davis's concern for liberty

        Conclusion

Jefferson Davis as President: A Confederate Asset

For many years after Robert E. Lee surrendered at Appomattox, historians tended to lay much of the blame for the South's crushing defeat upon the president of the Confederacy, Jefferson Davis. One writer, however, in comparing Davis to Lincoln, claims that Davis's reputation would have been quite different if he had been on the winning side. When a leader fails to achieve victory, even if his cause is doomed from the start, his "errors and defects and limitations of character . . . stand out as do a few spots of ink on a white sheet of paper."[1] This does not mean that Davis had no faults. Almost all historians agree that the man suffered from character flaws. He spent far too much time on administrative details, he often interfered in purely military matters, and he allowed himself to be drawn into bitter controversies with other political leaders. The question all Civil War analysts must answer is: To what extent did Davis's failings contribute to the defeat of the Confederacy? A survey of modern studies of Davis and the Civil War reveals a softening in the historical judgment of Davis as a leader. Most historians today conclude that Jefferson Davis, despite his personal shortcomings, was probably the most capable president the South could have chosen. Indeed, given the enormous

Introductory paragraph

Ellipsis

Question behind this research

Nature of sources

Thesis statement

2

problems the Confederacy faced, Davis was a
definite asset in the struggle to secede from the
Union.

Subtopic: Negative view of Davis

The most extreme negative criticism of
Jefferson Davis places the full weight of the
Southern defeat on his head. Edward A. Pollard, in
1869, took the view that the South, for the greater
part of the war, had the necessary resources,
morale, manpower, and military talent to defeat the
North. Thus, for Pollard, the cause of the South's
defeat "must come down by logical reduction to one
man--he the ruler who permitted these advantages to
be conquered through an imbecile and barren

Mixture of paraphrase and quotation

administration."[2] Pollard admitted that Davis
served the Southern cause with "distinguished
personal devotion," but he also claimed that Davis
destroyed this cause primarily through "his jealous
repulsion of advisers and assistants, and his
descent to rivalry in popularity with his
subordinates and lieutenants." In all, Pollard's
picture of Davis is of a man who combined strong
devotion to a cause with vanity and self-serving
ambition: a man who displayed a consistently
"puerile eagerness to appropriate all the honors of

One note covering several quotes

the Confederate cause and to wear them
conspicuously in the sight of the world."[3]

Pollard was a Southerner, a contemporary of
Davis, and a persistent critic of Davis throughout
the war.[4] His rather harsh evaluation of Davis,
written shortly after the war, may therefore
reflect not only his longstanding dislike of Davis

3

as a leader but also his dejection over the South's defeat. The need to find someone to blame for such a loss may have influenced other writers to accept, at least in part, Pollard's views. Rembert W. Patrick points out that the Confederate defeat "dimmed Davis's reputation for leadership." According to Patrick, the world often "fails to appreciate the quality of leadership that falls short of attaining the goal."[5]

A relatively modern evaluation of Davis presents a completely different view of the Confederate president than that of Pollard. "After years of investigation," Hudson Strode states, "I have concluded that one of Davis's most outstanding characteristics was his unselfishness, and it supported his integrity."[6] Strode prefers to attribute common human "flaws" to Davis rather than any special weaknesses of character or ability. He admits that, on occasion, Davis's "consciousness of intellectual superiority" made him appear to be "imperious." Further, because of his "genius" for getting to the heart of complex issues, "it was sometimes hard for Davis to delegate responsibility." In addition, Davis "was sensitive and somewhat thin-skinned, and he often made the mistake of answering his critics and wasting his time."[7]

Perhaps Strode's most significant point may be his conclusion that Davis lacked the gift for playing practical politics.

One note covering two quotes
Subtopic: Positive view of Davis

One note covering several quotes

4

Extended
quotation

He was not always conciliatory, and he
made enemies by letting his petitioners
know his opinion or decision at once, not
permitting them to go away still hoping
and maneuvering. . . . Davis was not formed
of elements that would make of him a
revolutionary dictator. He could not be
ruthless. . . . Therein, in the view of
some critics, he failed. Others believe
that he should have muzzled inimical
newspapers and jailed the editors,
because of the dissension and distrust
they created in the camps and on the home
front. But to Davis, the right of free
speech was fundamental.[8]

Student's
interpretation

Implied in this discussion of Davis's
political flaw is a comparison with Abraham
Lincoln's evident disregard for civil liberties. In
the North, some "inimical newspapers" were
"muzzled" and some editors jailed in the name of
eliminating unpatriotic dissension. William E.
Dodd, among others, makes this comparison directly:
"Davis was not indifferent to the personal liberty
of his people nor forgetful of the rights of

Support

individuals. . . . In this respect the contrast with
President Lincoln is all in favor of the Southern
leader."[9]

What emerges from Strode's discussion of Davis
is the picture of a noble leader who would not
compromise his integrity or treat civil liberties
lightly under the guise of emergency war powers.
Strode clearly favors a historical interpretation
of Davis's presidency that views him not as the
architect of the South's defeat, but as the devoted

5

leader whose "personal ability and determined
exercise of will . . . kept defeat off so long."[10]

　　Several other modern writers take a less
generous view of Davis's failings, but they agree
that he was an excellent choice for the presidency
and that the South stood no chance of winning the
war. Allan Nevins's evaluation of Davis's
presidency is less flattering than Strode's. He
faults Davis's performance as a leader on several
grounds. Davis, he argues, "overburdened himself
with details and overemphasized his military
responsibilities at the expense of his civil
functions." A still more damaging shortcoming was
Davis's "inability to labor amicably with other
men." His quarrels with some of his generals and
cabinet members could have been avoided, Nevins
claims, if the Confederate president had not
possessed "a natural disposition to quarrel" and
had been, instead, as "selfless, patient, and
generous as Abraham Lincoln."[11]

　　Nevins goes on to state, however, that in
spite of these shortcomings "Davis was
unquestionably the best man who could have been
chosen to guide the Confederacy". He bases this
judgment upon Davis's "vision," his "unshakable
integrity," his "large experience" in government,
and his "dignity in bearing and speech." These
strong points "constituted a greater body of assets
than any rival leader of the South could have
offered."[12]

　　J. G. Randall and David Donald agree with
Nevins that Jefferson Davis spent too much of his

Subtopic: One
moderate view of
Davis

One note covering
several quotes

Direct support of
the thesis
statement

One note covering
several quotes

Support for first
moderate view

6

time dealing with trivial matters and with strictly
military affairs. These historians find that Davis
took his constitutional duties as commander-in-
chief too seriously, causing him to become involved
with tactical considerations that were best left to
the military commanders in the field. Davis took
the position that "the President was entrusted with
military leadership, and he must exercise it."[13] In
their overview of his performance, however, Randall
and Donald balance their negative criticism of
Davis with a number of positive characteristics,
similar to those ascribed to him by Nevins. As a
final evaluation, they conclude that it was not any
individual flaw or combination of flaws that caused
Davis's failure but rather the enormity of the task

A secondary   he confronted. "Much of the criticism of the
aspect of thesis Confederate President fails to take into account
statement   the insuperable difficulties of his position and to
                      realize that no other Southern political leader
                      even approached Davis in stature."[14]

Subtopic: another   Another historian who has devoted many years
moderate view   and many volumes to the Civil War, Bruce Catton,
                      agrees that Davis's problems as president were
                      overwhelming. For one thing, he was faced at the
                      outset of his administration with the job of
                      preparing a new nation for war against an enemy
Support of thesis that possessed enormous advantages "in respect to
                      manpower, riches, and the commercial and industrial
                      strength that supports armies."[15] For another,
                      Davis was opposed continually by prominent
                      Southerners who were unable to share his vision of

7

a united Confederacy. "The administration had to
have broad wartime powers, but when Davis tried to
get and use them he was bitterly criticized."[16] On
this last point, Catton would seem to be expressing
agreement with the view that Davis was a leader
who, in order to do what was best for the whole
South, had to fight with those Southerners who
wanted only what they thought was best for
themselves or for their respective states. The
disastrous effects that this internal dissension
had on Davis's ability to lead are also emphasized
by Dodd. In writing of the objections to Davis's
policies voiced by men like Stephens and Joseph E.
Brown, the governor of Georgia during the war, Dodd
states that their opposition "must be pronounced as
a most important, if not the greatest, cause of the
final collapse of the Confederacy."[17]

Two sources
connected

His appreciation of the problems Davis had to
confront leads Catton to a final evaluation of
Davis's presidency that is close to that expressed
by Randall and Donald. Catton, however, also
suggests that Davis's attempt to lead his people to
independence was somehow doomed to failure from the
start.

> He had done the best he could do in an
> impossible job, and if it is easy to show
> where he made grievous mistakes, it is
> difficult to show that any other man,
> given the materials available, could have
> done much better. He had great courage,
> integrity, tenacity, devotion to his
> cause, and like Old Testament Sisera the
> stars in their courses marched against
> him.[18]

8

Subtopic: Davis's involvement in military affairs

Perhaps no defense of Jefferson Davis's presidency can be concluded without some reference to the most persistent criticism of his leadership. This criticism, mentioned by Randall and Donald as well as by Nevins, asserts that Davis was a "meddler" in military affairs, a frustrated former field commander whose interference in military tactics prevented the South from winning those major battles that might have discouraged the more powerful North from continuing the war. This criticism, however, may support Rembert Patrick's observation that history tends to underrate the positive qualities of a leader who fails to achieve a desired goal: the world also tends to exaggerate that leader's weaknesses. Certainly, there is ample evidence that Lincoln was just as much a meddler in strictly military affairs and equally prone to

Moderate view reaffirmed

making errors in military judgment. William L. Barney, for example, points out that Lincoln was constantly urging his generals to attack, despite the fact that the Union armies were often unprepared for bold advances and therefore suffered heavy casualties and gained no tactical advantages in doing so. "Slow to perceive the military realities of the war, Lincoln often made unreasonable demands."[19]

It is Barney's contention that neither Lincoln nor Davis nor, for that matter, the leading generals on either side, really understood the nature of a war that was being fought with thousands of men in the field, using weapons of an

9

advanced technology. "In fact, very few Civil War battles ever resulted in a decisive victory for either side. . . . The cost of battle was almost as high for the victor as for the defeated."[20] What finally brought victory to the North were not battlefield tactics. Victory came when the North used its superior resources and manpower to wage against the general population a war of attrition which ultimately destroyed the structure of Southern society. "To win its war of conquest, the Union turned to a theory of war that made civilians as well as armies its target."[21] In the light of Barney's analysis, therefore, it seems unfair to accuse Davis alone of being seriously flawed as a military leader. Apparently, the inability to direct armies to stunning battlefield victories was a "flaw" shared by the leadership on both sides in the Civil War.

> Student's
> judgment

As for the frequently expressed opinion that Davis had a "natural disposition to quarrel," there is evidence that the Confederate president's reputation for obstinacy was derived in large measure from his refusal to surrender his presidential prerogatives to men who believed states' rights and private interests ranked higher than the overall Confederate cause. One such man was the Confederacy's vice-president, Alexander H. Stephens. After about a year of active service to the Confederacy, Stephens withdrew to his native Georgia where he advocated a strong states' rights position and became an increasingly outspoken

> Quotation
> documented
> earlier
> Further support
> for moderate view
> of Davis
>
> Subtopic: Davis as
> a political leader

10

critic of Davis's policies. In tracing Davis's relationship with Stephens, James Z. Rabun leaves little doubt that the president's actions were almost always motivated by a genuine concern for the Southern cause, while Stephens's actions were almost always motivated by "self-righteousness" and narrow political concerns. As president, Davis "had given his loyalty to the South as a whole, and he was ready to sacrifice the supposed interests of any part to the attainment of the independence of the whole."[22] Rabun makes clear that much of the virulent criticism of Davis as a "dictator" and "tyrant" sprang from privileged Southerners who, like Stephens, were blind to the need to unite with Davis in the South's struggle for independence. Thus, Rabun's analysis of the quarrels between Stephens and Davis leads him to the conclusion that, far from being a dictator, "Davis gave ample evidence of loving liberty more dearly . . . than Stephens did."[23]

The results of this research into Jefferson Davis's presidency point strongly to the conclusion that Davis's major "error" consisted of accepting the leadership of a confederacy that was intent upon fighting a war that it had very little chance of winning. As a result, his name has become associated with the South's defeat, and his shortcomings as a leader have been emphasized in the light of that defeat. Undoubtedly, Davis had his fair share of weaknesses as a leader, but those weaknesses cannot reasonably explain the Confederacy's failure to achieve independence.

Summary of a source

Note referring to a periodical article

Conclusion: summary of the paper and restatement of the thesis

11

Along with his weaknesses, Davis had many strengths
as a leader, and these strengths were essential
ingredients in the South's ability to hold out for
so long against an enemy so superior in manpower
and resources. The Confederacy's only president
was, on balance, a devoted and able leader who,
faced with an impossible task, failed to perform a
miracle.

Notes

[1] Rembert W. Patrick, Jefferson Davis and His Cabinet (Baton Rouge: Louisiana State University Press, 1944), pp. 44–45.

[2] Edward A. Pollard, Life of Jefferson Davis, With a Secret History of the Southern Confederacy (1869; rpt. Freeport, N.Y.: Books for Libraries Press, 1969), p. 167.

[3] Pollard, p. 102.

[4] For a brief summary of Pollard vs. Davis, see Charles P. Roland, The Confederacy (Chicago: University of Chicago Press, 1960), pp. 55–56.

[5] Patrick, p. 44.

[6] Hudson Strode, Jefferson Davis: Tragic Hero (New York: Harcourt, Brace and World, 1964), p. xvi.

[7] Strode, p. xviii.

[8] Strode, pp. xviii–xix.

[9] William E. Dodd, Jefferson Davis (1907; rpt. New York: Russell and Russell, 1966), p. 291.

[10] Strode, p. xvi–xvii.

[11] Allan Nevins, The Organized War 1863–1864, vol. III of The War for the Union (New York: Scribner's, 1971), p. 37.

[12] Nevins, p. 39.

[13] J. G. Randall and David Donald, The Divided Union (Boston: Little, Brown, 1961), p. 271.

[14] Randall and Donald, p. 273.

[15] Bruce Catton, The Civil War (New York: American Heritage Press, 1971), p. 28.

[16] Catton, p. 220.

[17] Dodd, p. 268.

[18] Catton, p. 279.

[19] William L. Barney, Flawed Victory: A New Perspective on the Civil War (New York: Praeger, 1975), p. 9.

[20] Barney, pp. 7-8.

[21] Barney, p. 41.

[22] James Z. Rabun, "Alexander H. Stephens and Jefferson Davis," American Historical Review, 58 (1953), 301.

[23] Rabun, p. 321.

Bibliography

Barney, William L. Flawed Victory: A New Perspective
    on the Civil War. New York: Praeger, 1975.
Catton, Bruce. The Civil War. New York: American Heri-
    tage Press, 1971.
Dodd, William E. Jefferson Davis. 1907; rpt. New York:
    Russell and Russell, 1966.
Nevins, Allan. The Organized War 1863-64. Vol. III of
    The War for the Union. New York: Scribner's, 1971.
Patrick, Rembert W. Jefferson Davis and His Cabinet.
    Baton Rouge: Louisiana State University Press,
    1944.
Pollard, Edward A. Life of Jefferson Davis, With a Secret
    History of the Southern Confederacy, Gathered
    Behind the Scenes in Richmond. 1869; rpt. Free-
    port, N.Y.: Books for Libraries Press, 1969.
    Books for Libraries Press, 1969.
Rabun, James Z. "Alexander H. Stephens and Jefferson
    Davis." American Historical Review, 58 (1953), 301-
    24.
Randall, J. G., and David Donald. The Divided Union.
    Boston: Little, Brown, 1961.
Roland, Charles P. The Confederacy. Chicago: Univ. of
    Chicago Press, 1960.
Strode, Hudson. Jefferson Davis: Tragic Hero. New York:
    Harcourt, Brace and World, 1964.

Emily Dickinson's Reluctance to Publish

Submitted by Susanna Andrews
to Professor Ann Leigh

English 102 American Literature
Section 3c
June 2, 1981

```
                           OUTLINE
              Emily Dickinson's Reluctance to Publish


     Introductory paragraph, including thesis statement
       I. Background of the "myth of tragic Emily"
          A. Life in brief
             1. Retreat from social life
             2. Tentative effort to find an audience
             3. Eventual publication of her work
          B. After death
             1. The myth's genesis
             2. Its revision in recent years
          C. Refutation of "unworldly" image through
             analysis of poems
             1. The vocabulary (Thomas; Howard)
             2. The content (Griffith)
      II. The correspondence between Dickinson and Higginson
          A. The beginnings of their dialogue
             1. Higginson's article
             2. Dickinson's approach
          B. Higginson's first letter to the poet
             1. "Surgery" advised
             2. Request to see more poems
          C. Higginson's second letter
             1. Further revision advised
             2. Dickinson's response--disavowal of ambition
          D. Interpretations of Dickinson's reaction
             1. Disavowal questioned
             2. Higginson's blindness apparent
```

III. Dickinson's view of herself as an artist
    A. Her state of mind
        1. Self-confidence
        2. Realization that the world was not ready
        3. Refusal to compromise
    B. Dickinson's real reason for approaching
       Higginson
        1. Need for special kind of advice
        2. The painful first publications
    C. Higginson's effect on Emily Dickinson
        1. His limitations recognized
        2. His confusion in face of genius
        3. Her rejection of his advice
IV. Evidence from Dickinson's poetry
    A. Choice between fame and popular recognition
        1. Kher's interpretation of poem
        2. Poem's suggestion of her choice
    B. Choice between publication and artistic
       integrity
        1. Dickinson's decision to forgo publication
        2. Opposition of immortality and time

       Conclusion

Emily Dickinson's Reluctance to Publish

Introductory paragraph

Question behind this research

The traditional view

    At her death in 1886, Emily Dickinson left behind over 1700 poems, of which only seven were published——anonymously——while she was alive.[1] Certainly then, the woman Yvor Winters called "one of the greatest lyric poets of all time"[2] was all but unknown as a poet during her lifetime. For many years after her poems first appeared in 1890, her reluctance to publish was attributed to a supposed unconcern for worldly matters, including literary fame. Literary critics, serious biographers, and writers of fictionalized accounts of her life created an image of Emily Dickinson as a timid, reclusive, mystical thinker, who was too absorbed in personal sorrows and ecstasies to be concerned with literary recognition. And this image persists, to a great extent, in the public mind today.[3] Since

    [1] Thomas H. Johnson, ed., The Poems of Emily Dickinson (Cambridge: The Belknap Press, Harvard University Press, 1955), I, lx.

    [2] Yvor Winters, "Emily Dickinson and the Limits of Judgment," in Emily Dickinson: A Collection of Critical Essays, ed. Richard B. Sewall (Englewood Cliffs, N.J.: Prentice-Hall, 1963), p. 40.

    [3] For a discussion of sources leading to the "Emily myth," see Paul J. Ferlazzo, Emily Dickinson (Boston: Twayne, 1976), pp. 13–21.

the late 1950s, however, a new view of the poet has
been emerging. This view, based on close studies of
Dickinson's life, letters, and poetry, reveals an
artist well aware of her worth who deliberately
chose to withhold her poems from the world until
they could be valued as unique artistic creations,
even if this meant postponing fame until after her
death.

    Beginning in her midtwenties, Emily Dickinson
gradually retreated from the many stimulating
personal relationships that had filled her early
life. By her late thirties, her retirement was
complete; she passed the rest of her days living
with her parents and her younger sister, who
managed the household. During her later years,
Emily Dickinson had virtually no direct contact
with anyone outside her immediate family. While she
was still connected to her circle of friends,
Dickinson made at least one tentative attempt to
find an audience for her poetry. But only a handful
of verses were published anonymously, most of them
in a local newspaper, and these were subjected to
considerable editing. Upon the poet's death at
fifty-six, her sister discovered over one thousand
poems and initiated an effort to publish them.
Beginning four years later, in 1890, these poems
finally appeared in print.[4]

    [4] Richard B. Sewall, <u>The Life of Emily Dickinson</u>
(New York: Farrar, Straus and Giroux, 1974), I, 4–
11.

Marginal annotations:

- Nature of sources
- Thesis statement
- Subtopic: background of the myth
- Summary of a source

3

Over the years, as her following grew, Emily
Dickinson became the subject of a number of highly
romanticized biographies. Her admirers were trying
to establish a connection between her cloistered
existence and the powerful passions that course
through much of her finest poetry. Only after
scholarly editions of her letters and poetry
appeared in the 1950s were literary critics in a
good position to produce an accurate picture of the
poet's life and her attitude toward her art. Even
so, a good deal of the mystery remains with us.

Subtopic:
refutation of myth

The idea that Emily Dickinson knew very little
of the real world has been disputed by recent
studies of her life and works. One biographer and
critic, Owen Thomas, finds a remarkable number of
legal, political, and financial words and
expressions in her poetry. This fact leads him to
conclude that Dickinson "was well aware of the
world outside her little room, that in fact she
used the language of this outside world to create
some of her best poetry."[5] In the same vein,
William Howard points out that the largest group of
specialized words in Dickinson's poems reflects the
scientific and technological discussions of her
day.[6] Further disagreement with the image of the

[5] Owen Thomas, "Father and Daughter: Edward and
Emily Dickinson," _American Literature_, 40 (1969),
523.
[6] William Howard, "Emily Dickinson's Poetic
Vocabulary," _PMLA_, 72 (1957), 230.

poet as a shy, unworldly creature come from Clark
Griffith, who sees her as a person whose
sensibility was "responsive to the brutalities
which life imposes on the individual, and acutely
aware of the nothingness with which existence
appears surrounded."[7] If we reject the image of
Emily Dickinson as a mystical recluse who had
little interest in the real world, we must also
question the theory that she did not publish her
poems out of the same lack of interest.

Connection with thesis

Perhaps the most substantial evidence
regarding Dickinson's reluctance to publish can be
found in her letters to a professional writer and
social reformer named Thomas Wentworth Higginson.
This correspondence began in 1862, after Higginson
published an article in the April issue of the
Atlantic Monthly, entitled "Letter to a Young
Contributor," which offered some practical advice
for beginning writers seeking to publish. As a
result of reading this article, Dickinson sent
Higginson four poems, along with a letter
containing this question: "Are you too deeply
occupied to say if my Verse is alive?"[8] This and
other early letters in their correspondence reveal
the poet's interest in gaining recognition. Later

Subtopic:
correspondence
with Higginson

Reference to
primary source

___

[7] Clark Griffith, The Long Shadow: Emily
Dickinson's Tragic Poetry (Princeton: Princeton
University Press, 1964), pp. 5–6.
    [8] The Letters of Emily Dickinson, ed. Thomas H.
Johnson and Theodora Ward (Cambridge, Mass.:
Harvard University Press, 1958), II, 403.

5

correspondence with Higginson seems, however, to
have dampened her hope of achieving critical
praise.

    Unfortunately, almost all of Higginson's
letters to Emily Dickinson have been lost.
Nevertheless, the main points of his answers to her
early letters have been inferred by numerous
critics, using the poet's replies to Higginson as
the basis for these conclusions. Paul Ferlazzo, for
example, infers that Higginson's response to her
first letter must have included some
recommendations for altering, or "regularizing,"
her poems, along with a request for more of her
work.[9] Ferlazzo bases this judgment on Dickinson's
second letter to Higginson, which says, in part,
"Thank you for the surgery--it was not so painful
as I supposed. I bring you others--as you ask--
though they might not differ--"[10] The "surgery"
surely refers to some changes recommended by
Higginson, and Ferlazzo thinks it is significant
that the poet admits she is sending him more poems
of the same kind, for this indicates that she did
not intend to follow his advice.[11]

Support for thesis   In a second letter to Dickinson, Higginson
must have recommended that she not try to publish
for the present time, perhaps suggesting that she
rewrite her poems along the lines he had

    [9] Ferlazzo, p. 136.
    [10] _Letters_, II, 404.
    [11] Ferlazzo, p. 137.

6

prescribed. This can be inferred from her reply to
this letter, which reads, in part:

> I smile when you suggest that I delay "to
> publish"--that being foreign to my
> thought, as Firmament to Fin--
> If fame belonged to me, I could not
> escape her--if she did not, the longest
> day would pass me on the chase--
> . . . My Barefoot--Rank is better.[12]

Those critics who believe that Dickinson's
reluctance to publish was a deliberate choice on
her part do not take at face value her avowal to
Higginson that publishing was "foreign" to her.
Instead, they see Higginson's inability to
recognize the genius in her work as a major factor
in her decision to renounce her desire to publish.
As Richard Sewall says it, Dickinson's

> . . . disavowal about publishing can
> hardly be taken literally. After all, she
> had sent him [Higginson] the poems in
> response to his article on how young
> writers could get their work published.
> . . . What she said . . . about publishing
> could perhaps mean that, in view of
> Higginson's hesitance, she was renouncing
> her ambition to be a public poet . . .
> perhaps in the hope that some far-off
> Tribunal would render different and
> unequivocal judgment. . . .[13]

Extended quotation; student felt it was necessary to identify "him" in brackets

In suggesting that Dickinson chose obscurity

---

[12] Letters, II, 408.
[13] Sewall, II, 554.

7

Subtopic:
Dickinson's view
of herself as an
artist

Support for thesis

Two sources
connected

after Higginson's "hesitance," Sewall does not mean
to imply that she was made unsure of herself as a
poet because of his criticisms. On the contrary,
Sewall states that "in her exalted conception of
herself as a poet and in her confidence in her
powers, she had no . . . reason to be deferential to
Higginson . . . and one cannot help feeling that she
knew it."[14] Thus, it was not a sense of inferiority
that moved the poet to her decision. Rather it was
the realization that her poems would not be
accepted in the forms she had created for them and
that public recognition would require her to alter
them to meet popular expectations. Robert Spiller,
in finding that Dickinson "failed to publish"
because she would not accept compromise as a path
to recognition, makes much the same point as
Sewall:

> "The general reading public that asked
> for meter that is smooth, rhythm that is
> easy, and words that are limited to only
> one obvious meaning interested her not at
> all. She was willing to wait."[15]

In this same regard, Johnson remarks that,
although Dickinson's early letters to Higginson do
indicate an interest in publication, she is also

---

[14] Sewall, II, 555.
[15] Robert E. Spiller, The Cycle of American
Literature: An Essay in Historical Criticism, 2nd
ed. (New York: Free Press, 1967), p. 127.

8

asking for a special kind of advice. "At the time she wrote Higginson," Johnson explains, "she does not seem to be trying to avoid publication as such; she is inquiring how one can publish and at the same time preserve the integrity of one's art." This inquiry, Johnson continues, was a real concern for Dickinson because prior to her writing to Higginson, two of her poems had been published anonymously in the <u>Springfield Daily Republican</u>, an influential newspaper of that time, and both poems had been altered radically by editors to suit their sense of regularity.[16]

Modern critics and biographers are in almost universal agreement that she was disappointed in Higginson's response to her poetry. They also agree that she decided very early in her correspondence that, as Ferlazzo puts it, the man "lacked discernment as to her purpose as an artist."[17] Thomas Johnson, in his appraisal of their correspondence, concludes that Higginson, though somewhat impressed by the wording and thoughts in Dickinson's poems, "literally did not understand what he was reading." By this, Johnson means that Higginson was confronted with the work of an "original genius" and was bewildered as to what to make of it.[18] Throughout his correspondence with

[16] Thomas H. Johnson, <u>Emily Dickinson: An Interpretative Biography</u> (Cambridge, Mass.: Harvard University Press, 1955), p. 11.

[17] Ferlazzo, p. 139.

[18] Johnson, <u>Biography</u>, p. 111.

Mixture of paraphrase and quotation

Mixture of paraphrase and quotation

her, Higginson was apparently attempting to get her to write more traditional poetry, or, as Johnson observes: "He was trying to measure a cube by the rules of plane geometry."[19] There is no evidence, however, that she ever followed any of Higginson's suggestions, despite the fact that she maintained a friendly correspondence with him for many years.

Subtopic: evidence from poetry

For Emily Dickinson, then, the idea of revising her creations for the sake of achieving quick--and probably fleeting--recognition was what was "foreign" to her, not recognition based on acceptance of her poems as unique works of art. This conviction comes through clearly in several of her poems; for example:

Reference to primary source

>   Fame is the one that does not stay--
>   Its occupant must die
>   Or out of sight of estimate
>   Ascend incessantly--
>   Or be that most insolvent thing
>   A Lightning in the Germ--
>   Electrical the embryo
>   But we demand the Flame.[20]

Support for thesis

In commenting on this poem, Inder Nath Kher says that it does not mean that Dickinson is "averse to genuine fame." It means, he continues, "that she does not wish to be considered as writing

[19] Johnson, _Biography_, p. 107.
[20] _The Complete Poems of Emily Dickinson_, ed. Thomas H. Johnson (Boston: Little, Brown, 1960), pp. 623-24.

10

simply for the sake of some cheap glory."21
Reinforced by this poem--assuming "we" in the last
refers to the poet--is the conclusion that
Dickinson would rather have had "the Flame" of her
artistic integrity than the "insolvent thing"
called popular recognition.

    Along the same lines, given her deliberate
decision to forgo publication rather than
compromise her art, the first lines of another poem
become significantly clear: "Publication--is the
Auction / Of the Mind of Man."22 And there can be
no doubt that when she wrote the following stanza,
Emily Dickinson had accepted the fact that true
fame would not be hers in her lifetime.

> Some--Work for Immortality--
> The Chiefer part, for Time--
> He--Compensates--immediately
> The former--Checks--on Fame--23

She chose to maintain her artistic integrity and
await that immortality.

    The personality of Emily Dickinson will
continue to fascinate those who enjoy speculating
about brilliant artists whose lives were cloaked in
privacy. Since she said so little about herself

References to primary sources

Support for thesis

Conclusion

---

21 Inder Nath Kher, The Landscape of Absence:
Emily Dickinson's Poetry (New Haven: Yale University
Press, 1974), p. 128.

22 Complete Poems, pp. 348-49.

23 Complete Poems, p. 193.

outside of her somewhat enigmatic poetry and her
letters, the popular image of a mystical, romantic
Emily is likely to coexist for many years with
scholarly appraisals of her life and work. Her
poetry, however, does more than create an aura of
mystery about its author; it reveals a dedicated
genius moved by a deep, religious reverence for her
Restatement of craft. Yet Emily Dickinson, gifted with the power
the thesis to create extraordinary works of art, also felt
compelled to preserve the uniqueness of her
creations by refusing to compromise in order to
attain public recognition. She was willing to trust
that future generations of readers would award her
the fame her work deserved.

Bibliography

Dickinson, Emily. The Complete Poems of Emily
    Dickinson. Ed. Thomas H. Johnson. Boston:
    Little, Brown, 1960.
----------. The Letters of Emily Dickinson.
    Ed. Thomas H. Johnson and Theodora Ward.
    3 vols. Cambridge, Mass.: Harvard
    University Press, 1958.
----------. The Poems of Emily Dickinson. Ed.
    Thomas H. Johnson. 3 vols. Cambridge: The
    Belknap Press, Harvard University Press,
    1955.
Ferlazzo, Paul J. Emily Dickinson. Boston:
    Twayne, 1976.
Griffith, Clark. The Long Shadow: Emily
    Dickinson's Tragic Poetry. Princeton:
    Princeton Univ. Press, 1964.
Howard, William. "Emily Dickinson's Poetic
    Vocabulary." PMLA, 72 (1957), 225–48.
Johnson, Thomas H. Emily Dickinson: An
    Interpretative Biography. Cambridge: Har-
    vard Univ. Press, 1955.
--- --------, ed. The Complete Poems of Emily
    Dickinson. Boston: Little, Brown, 1960.
Kher, Inder Nath. The Landscape of Absence: Emily
    Dickinson's Poetry. New Haven: Yale Univ.
    Press, 1974.

Johnson as author precedes Johnson as editor. Title is listed twice because both Johnson and Dickinson are cited in the text

Sewall, Richard B. <u>The Life of Emily Dickinson</u>. 2
    vols. New York: Farrar, Straus and Giroux,
    1974.
Spiller, Robert E. <u>The Cycle of American
    Literature: An Essay in Historical
    Criticism</u>. 2nd ed. New York: Free Press, 1967.
Thomas, Owen. "Father and Daughter: Edward and
    Emily Dickinson." <u>American Literature</u>,   40
    (1960), 510–23.
Winters, Yvor. "Emily Dickinson and the Limits of
    Judgment." In <u>Emily Dickinson: A Collection
    of Critical Essays</u>. Ed. Richard B. Sewall.
    Englewood Cliffs, N.J.: Prentice–Hall, 1963.

Index

Afterwords
  in bibliographies, 139
  in footnotes, 144
Architecture, sources on, 21, 51
Art, sources on, 8, 21, 51
Astronomy, sources on, 21, 51
Audiovisual material
  in libraries, 48–49
  *See also specific types of audiovisual
    material*
Author card of library card catalog, 33–35
Authority, quoting for, 79, 81
Author/year system of documentation,
  150–156

Background reading, 8–9, 18, 26–29
Balanced outlines, 114
*Bibliographical Index: A Cumulative
  Bibliography of Bibliographies,* 47
Bibliographies
  general, 50–54
  source documentation with, 135–142
  See also Working bibliographies
Bibliography cards, 57–59, 65
Biographies, sources on, 8, 9, 21–22, 51
Biology
  forms of lists of references for, 153
  sources on, 22, 51
Book Review Digest, The, 39, 45, 56
Botany, forms of lists of references for, 153
Brainstorming, 7–8, 18
Business, sources on, 22, 51

Call slips, 38
  number of, on bibliography cards, 58
Card catalog of library, 33–36
Chemistry
  forms of lists of references for, 154
  sources on, 22, 51
Closed stacks of books, 38
College libraries, 31–56
  card catalog of, 33–36
  kinds of sources available in (*See specific
    types of sources*)
Context, quoting in, 82

Corporate publications
  in bibliographies, 139
  in footnotes, 145
Corrections, on final manuscript, 161
Coverage, extent of, in books or articles,
  65–66

Diaries, in libraries, 33
Documentation of sources, 4, 131–158
  author/year system of, 150–156
  basic information provided by, 134
  with bibliographies, 135–142
  with footnotes, 142–149
  for illustrative materials, 149–150
  numbered system of, 152–155
  where necessary, 132–134
Drafts
  final, 130
  rough, 120–129
Drama, sources on, 22, 51

Economics
  forms of lists of references for, 155
  sources on, 22, 52
Edition number
  in bibliographies, 139, 140
  in footnotes, 145
Editor's comments
  in bibliographies, 139
  in footnotes, 145
Education
  forms of lists of references for, 155
  sources on, 22, 52
Ellipsis, 84
Encyclopedia articles
  in bibliographies, 140
  in footnotes, 145–146
Encyclopedias, 8, 9, 21
Endnotes. *See* Footnotes
Engineering
  forms of lists of references for, 154
  sources on, 23, 52
English. *See* Language
Enlarged edition
  in bibliographies, 139
  in footnotes, 145

Environmental science, sources on, 23, 52
Essays, 2
  in bibliographies, 136
  in footnotes, 143
Ethnic studies, sources on, 52
Explanations, documenting personal, 132, 133

Facts and factual information, 132–134
  gathered by observers, need to document, 132, 134
  open to dispute, need to document, 132, 133
Films
  in bibliographies, 141
  in footnotes, 146
Final draft, 130
Final manuscript, 159–161
  samples of, 161–194
Footnotes (endnotes), 142–149
  format for, 147–149
  short forms, 147
Forewords
  in bibliographies, 139
  in footnotes, 144

General bibliographies, 50–54
General encyclopedias, 21
General sources, 21–25, 50–54
  for background reading, 8, 9
Geology, forms of lists of references for, 154
Government agency publications
  in bibliographies, 139
  in footnotes, 145

Health education, sources on, 52
History
  forms of lists of references for, 155
  sources on, 23, 53
Humanities Index, 46
Hypothesis, 4
  defined, 2
  formation of, 18–20
  revising, 62, 63

Illustrative materials, documenting, 149–150
Indexes
  to periodicals, 38–47, 50–54
  vertical file, 48
Interlibrary loans, 49

Interviews, 50
Introductory paragraph, 110–112

Journals
  evaluating articles of, 69
  representative, listed, 50–54
  See also specific types of journals

Language
  sources on, 23, 53
Law, sources on, 53
Lectures
  in bibliographies, 140
  in footnotes, 146
Letters
  in libraries, 33
  requesting interviews, 50
  small and capital, in outlines, 114
Libraries
  and working with librarians, 31–32
  other than college libraries, 49
  (see also College libraries)
Library of Congress, 37
Linguistics, sources on, 23
Lists of references, forms of, for disciplines other than humanities, 153–156
Literary works, footnotes to, 148–149
Literature, sources on, 23–24, 53
Loans, interlibrary, 49

Magazines. See Periodicals
Main idea (topic) sentence, 125
Manuscripts
  in libraries, 33
  preparation of final, 4, 159–161
Margins and spacing, on final manuscript, 160
Mathematics, forms of lists of references for, 154
Media
  sources on, 24
  See also Periodicals; Radio programs; Television programs
Microforms, in libraries, 33, 48
Monthly Catalog (U.S. Government Printing Office), 49
Museum libraries, 49
Music, sources on, 24, 53

Newspaper Index, 45
Newspapers. See Periodicals

New York Public Library, 49
New York Times Index, 39, 42–44, 56
Notebooks, 73
Note cards, 73
  entering information on, 73–75
  entering quotations on, 84–86
  sorting, and preparing to write paper,
    107–108
Note-taking, 3, 72–106
  copying and, 75–76
  example of effective, 86–97
  paraphrasing and, 76–77, 82–84
  plagiarism and, 97–101
  practical aspects of, 72–75
  quoting and, 76, 79–86
  and source evaluation, 66
  summarizing and, 77–79
  when skimming through periodicals, 65
Numbered documentation system, 152–155
Numbers and numbering
  in outlines, 114
  placement of footnote numbers in text, 149

Obsolete sources, 67–68
Official testimonies
  in bibliographies, 140
  in footnotes, 146
Outlines, 110–117
  balanced, 114
  format for, 114–117

Page numbering, on final manuscript, 160
Pamphlets, unsigned
  in bibliographies, 140
  in footnotes, 146
Paragraphs
  introductory, 110–112
  revising, 125
Paraphrasing, 76–77, 82–84
Periodicals
  defined, 32
  documenting articles from, 137–138,
    143–144
  evaluating articles of, 68, 69
  indexes to, 38–47, 50–54
  information on articles of, on
    bibliography cards, 58–59
  locating, in library, 47
  skimming through, 65
  types of, 39
  See also Journals
Philosophy, sources on, 24, 54

Physical education, sources on, 52
Physics
  forms of lists of references for, 154–155
  sources on, 24, 54
Pictorial material, in libraries, 33
Plagiarism, 97–101
Political science
  forms of lists of references for, 155
  sources on, 24–25, 54
Poole's Index to Periodical Literature, 40
Prefaces
  in bibliographies, 139
  in footnotes, 144
Preliminary research, 3–4
Primary sources, 68
Printed materials, special, 49
Professional journals, 39, 46–47
Professional societies, libraries of, 49
Psychology
  forms of lists of references for, 155–156
  sources on, 25, 54
Public Broadcasting System (PBS), 49
Public libraries, 49

Questionnaires, preparing, 50
Quoting, 76, 79–86

Radio programs, 49–50
Reader's Guide to Periodical Literature, The,
    39–42, 56
Reading
  as part of preliminary research, 3–4
  See also Background reading; Note-
    taking; *and specific reading material*
Reading room, reserved, 38
Recordings
  in bibliographies, 141
  in footnotes, 147
  in libraries, 33
Reference sources. *See* Sources
Religion, sources on, 25, 54
Reprinted edition
  in bibliographies, 140
  in footnotes, 145
Reserve books, 38
Reserve reading room, 38
Reviews of other works
  in bibliographies, 139
  in footnotes, 145
Revised edition
  in bibliographies, 139
  in footnotes, 145

Revision, of rough drafts, 123–129
Roman numerals, in outlines, 114
Rough drafts, 120–129

Scholarly journals, 39, 46–47
Sciences
    forms of lists of references for, 153–155
    See also specific sciences
Secondary sources, 68
Sentence outlines, 117
Sentences, revising, 125–127
Skimming, 63–65
Social sciences
    forms of lists of references for, 155–156
    The Reader's Guide to Periodical Literature
        for, 40
    Social Sciences Index, 46
    See also specific social sciences
Social Sciences Index, 46, 56
Sociology, sources on, 25, 54
Sound recordings. *See* Recordings
Sources, 57–71
    and compilation of working
        bibliography, 57–59, 61–63
    documenting. *See* Documentation of
        sources
    evaluating potential, 65–69
    finding, 3 (*See also* Libraries)
    gathering, 59–61
    general (*See* General sources)
    integration of, 121–123
    reading (*See* Note-taking)
Spacing and margins, on final manuscript,
    160
Specialized collections, 33, 48
Specialized indexes, 46–47
Specialized journals, 51, 52, 54
Special printed materials, obtaining, 49
Subject, 4
    defined, 2
    objective definition and choice of, 5–6
Subject cards, of library card catalog, 33–
    35
Subtopics
    arranging note-taking information by,
        73, 74

in introductory paragraph, 110
    in outline, 113–114
Summarizing, 77–79
Surveys, preparing, 50
Synonyms, dictionary of, 129

Television programs, 49–50
    in bibliographies, 141
    in footnotes, 146
Testimonies. *See* Official testimonies
Theories, documenting, 132, 133
Thesaurus (book of synonyms), 129
Thesis
    arriving at, 3–4
    defined, 2
    determining, by self-questioning, 108–
        110
    in introductory paragraph, 110
Title card, of library card catalog, 33, 34,
    36
Title page, of final manuscript, 160
Topic, 4
    choice of, 6–18
    defined, 2
    reassessing one's, following
        bibliography compilation, 61–63
Topic (main idea) sentence, 125
Transcriptions, of television and radio
    programs, 50

United States Government Printing Office
    (GPO), 49
Unpublished material, in libraries, 33

Vertical file index, 48

Women, sources on, 54
Working bibliographies
    compilation of, 57–59
    need for variety of viewpoints in, 67
    reassessing one's topic following
        compilation of, 61–63

Zoology, forms of lists of references for,
    153